IN MEMORIAM

broadview editions
series editor: L.W. Conolly

Richard Doyle, pencil drawing of Tennyson around 1855. Courtesy of Princeton University Library.

IN MEMORIAM

Alfred Tennyson

edited by Matthew Rowlinson

broadview editions

Library and Archives Canada Cataloguing in Publication

Tennyson, Alfred Tennyson, Baron, 1809-1892, author
   In memoriam / Alfred Tennyson ; edited by Matthew Rowlinson.

(Broadview editions)
Includes bibliographical references.
ISBN 978-1-55481-143-4 (pbk.)

   1. Hallam, Arthur Henry, 1811-1833—Poetry. 2. Tennyson, Alfred Tennyson, Baron, 1809-1892. In memoriam. I. Rowlinson, Matthew, 1956-, editor II. Title. III. Series: Broadview editions

PR5562.A2R69 2014   821'.8   C2014-903215-3

Broadview Editions

The Broadview Editions series represents the ever-changing canon of literature in English by bringing together texts long regarded as classics with valuable lesser-known works.

Advisory editor for this volume: Juliet Sutcliffe

Broadview Press is an independent, international publishing house, incorporated in 1985.

We welcome comments and suggestions regarding any aspect of our publications— please feel free to contact us at the addresses below or at broadview@broadviewpress.com.

North America
Post Office Box 1243, Peterborough, Ontario K9J 7H5, Canada
555 Riverwalk Parkway, Tonawanda, NY 14150, USA
Tel: (705) 743-8990; Fax: (705) 743-8353
email: customerservice@broadviewpress.com

UK, Europe, Central Asia, Middle East, Africa, India, and Southeast Asia
Eurospan Group, 3 Henrietta St., London WC2E 8LU, United Kingdom
Tel: 44 (0) 1767 604972; Fax: 44 (0) 1767 601640
email: eurospan@turpin-distribution.com

Australia and New Zealand
NewSouth Books
c/o TL Distribution, 15-23 Helles Ave., Moorebank, NSW 2170, Australia
Tel: (02) 8778 9999; Fax: (02) 8778 9944
email: orders@tldistribution.com.au

www.broadviewpress.com

Broadview Press acknowledges the financial support of the Government of Canada through the Canada Book Fund for our publishing activities.

Typesetting and assembly: True to Type Inc., Claremont, Canada.

PRINTED IN CANADA

Contents

Acknowledgements • 7
Introduction • 9
Alfred Tennyson: A Brief Chronology • 31
A Note on the Text • 35

In Memoriam • 37

Appendix A: Writings of Arthur Hallam • 147
  1. Meditative Fragment 1 (1829) • 147
  2. Sonnet [After first meeting Emily Tennyson] (1829) • 149
  3. Sonnet [The garden trees] (1831) • 149
  4. From "On Sympathy" (1830) • 149

Appendix B: Writings on Natural History, Taxonomy, and
        Evolution, 1802–44 • 157
  1. From William Paley, *Natural Theology; or, Evidences of the
     Existence and Attributes of the Deity* (1802) • 157
  2. From Charles Lyell, *The Principles of Geology*, Vol. 1
     (1830) • 160
  3. From Robert Chambers, *Vestiges of the Natural History of
     Creation* (1844) • 165

Appendix C: Victorian Courtship and Marriage in Fiction • 169
  1. From Mary Russell Mitford, *Our Village: Sketches of Rural
     Character and Scenery* (1824) • 169
  2. From Charles Dickens, *David Copperfield* (1850) • 172

Appendix D: The Poetic Sequence, 1827–54 • 179
  1. From John Keble, *The Christian Year: Thoughts in Verse for
     the Sundays and Holidays Throughout the Year* (1827) • 179
  2. From Elizabeth Barrett Browning, *Sonnets from the
     Portuguese* (1850) • 184
  3. From Coventry Patmore, *The Angel in the House:
     The Betrothal* (1854) • 187

Appendix E: Reviews of *In Memoriam*, 1850–55 • 193
  1. From [John Forster?], *The Examiner* (8 June 1850) • 193
  2. From *The Literary Gazette* (15 June 1850) • 194
  3. From *The North British Review* (August 1850) • 194
  4. From *The Eclectic Review* (September 1850) • 194
  5. From *The English Review* (September 1850) • 195
  6. From [Charles Kingsley], *Fraser's Magazine* (September
     1850) • 197

7. From [Manley Hopkins?], *The Times* (28 November 1851) • 198
8. From [Coventry Patmore], *The Edinburgh Review* (October 1855) • 199

Appendix F: From Hallam Tennyson, *Alfred Lord Tennyson: A Memoir by His Son* (1897) • 203

Select Bibliography • 205

Acknowledgements

This edition has been shaped by my experience teaching *In Memoriam*, and I am grateful to all of the students at Dartmouth College and the University of Western Ontario who over the years have allowed me to share Tennyson's strange and moving poem with them. I am also grateful to the University of Western Ontario for the award of a Faculty Scholarship from 2011 to 2013, which provided invaluable funding.

The edition would not exist without my research assistants, Pascale McCullough Manning and Meghan O'Hara, who corrected innumerable errors of substance and format. I was especially fortunate in being able to rely on Dr. Manning's expertise in the history of nineteenth-century science when selecting the excerpts in Appendix B, for which she composed the headnotes.

Like anyone who works on *In Memoriam*, I am indebted to the lasting scholarship of A.C. Bradley's *Commentary on Tennyson's In Memoriam* (3rd ed., 1910), of Christopher Ricks's *The Poems of Tennyson* (1987), and of Susan Shatto and Marion Shaw's variorum edition (1982). In introducing and annotating the poem, I have used their work throughout; this blanket acknowledgement will I hope serve instead of individual references that would otherwise appear on nearly every page.

Parts of the introduction are excerpted from my essay "History, Materiality, and Type in Tennyson's *In Memoriam*" (in Valerie Purton, ed., *Darwin, Tennyson and their Readers: Explorations in Literature and Science* [London: Anthem, 2013], 35–48). I am grateful for the permission of Anthem Press to adapt this material here. I am also grateful to the Thomas Fisher Rare Books library at the University of Toronto for providing the photograph of *In Memoriam*'s first edition title page that appears on p. 37; the original drawing of Tennyson reproduced on the frontispiece belongs to Princeton University Library. I am grateful to both libraries for providing images and permitting the reproduction of items from their holdings.

Introduction

In Memoriam's Origins and Composition

Alfred Tennyson and Arthur Hallam met at Cambridge, where they were both students at Trinity College. Tennyson was the elder by 18 months, but in many ways the less worldly of the two friends, having grown up in a rural parsonage in the east-coast county of Lincolnshire, where he was educated almost entirely at home by his father, the rector of Somersby. Hallam was the son of a celebrated historian whose inherited wealth enabled the family to maintain their home in London and spend summers in the country; he was educated at Eton College. He matriculated at Cambridge in the fall of 1828, a year after Tennyson, and the two met sometime that year. In the spring of 1829 they both entered poems in competition for the Chancellor's Gold Medal in poetry, which Tennyson won.

By the fall the two were fast friends: they had both been elected to an undergraduate literary society known as the Apostles. Hallam rapidly emerged as an intellectual leader in the group; Appendix A4 of this edition (p. 149) excerpts a paper, "On Sympathy," that he read to them in 1830. Tennyson never succeeded in finishing a paper for the Apostles; in consequence he lost his formal membership, though he continued to attend the society's meetings, and its members were the first audience for the important poems he wrote in this period, including "Mariana," "The Lady of Shalott," and "The Palace of Art." By the end of 1829 Hallam and Tennyson were planning to publish their poems in a joint volume, for which Hallam had found a publisher. When Hallam's father vetoed this plan, the volume came out with Tennyson as sole author; Hallam was able to use his literary connections to place a long review in the August 1831 issue of the up and coming young publisher Edward Moxon's new *Englishman's Magazine* (1: 616–28).

Together with the circle of friends that formed around the two of them, Arthur Hallam managed Tennyson's emergence as a professional poet. The publication of Tennyson's second solo volume, which appeared in 1832, was also arranged by Hallam. This volume was brought out by Moxon, whose firm was to publish Tennyson's poetry, including *In Memoriam*, until 1869.

In December 1829 Hallam made what was to be the first of many visits to the Tennyson family at Somersby; at this time he met Tennyson's sister Emily, to whom he later became engaged. In the summer of 1830 the two men traveled to the south of France together. It was Tennyson's first trip outside England; the hot, dry, mountainous landscape of the French Pyrenees was to haunt poems of erotic longing he wrote in the aftermath, such as "Fatima," "Oenone," and "The Hesperides." On this trip the two of them carried dispatches and money to Constitutionalist insurgents against the Spanish monarchy. They brought support to the insurgents from British liberals, including some recently graduated members of the Apostles. Tennyson was put off by the violent language of the Spanish guerillas when they met on the French side of the border; we have no record of his response to the insurgency's disastrous end the following year with the failure of an attempted invasion and the execution of the leaders, including their British supporter Robert Boyd.[1]

Tennyson left Cambridge in 1831 without taking a degree; his father's death that year made it financially impossible to continue. During the summer of 1832 he and Hallam made a second European trip, this time up the Rhine to Germany. By this time Hallam was engaged to Emily; his father disapproved and there was acrimonious correspondence between him and Emily's trustee about money. Hallam spent the Christmas of 1832 at Somersby; in 1833 he graduated and moved to London to prepare for a legal career, and in the late summer embarked on a trip to Austria and Eastern Europe with his father. He was not to return: on 15 September he died of a cerebral aneurysm in his hotel room in Vienna. The Tennyson family received the news at Somersby in the beginning of October. The return of the body by ship, which Tennyson describes in the first-written sections of *In Memoriam*, took until December; Hallam was buried at Clevedon, Somerset on 3 January 1834. Tennyson did not attend, nor does he appear to have visited the grave until 1850, in the immediate aftermath of *In Memoriam*'s publication and of his ensuing marriage to Emily Sellwood.

Hallam's death thus deprived Tennyson of a friend in whom many hopes were bound up. His entire circle had expected Hallam to have a brilliant career. For Tennyson, his closest friend, he had been the reader whose belief in the poet's work and whose metropolitan connections made it possible for him to publish. After Hallam's death Tennyson continued to write, but he was

---

1 For details of this episode, see A.J. Sambrook, "Cambridge Apostles at a Spanish Tragedy," *English Miscellany* 16 (1965): 183–94.

not to publish another volume until 1842. Moreover, especially after his mother left Somersby in 1837, he took up a restless and unsettled life in which he moved frequently and spent long periods visiting friends, usually from the old days at Cambridge. Throughout this time he worked on the elegies—untitled until just before their publication—that eventually became *In Memoriam*.

The first-written sections of the poem date from the weeks after Tennyson heard of Hallam's death: they are sections 9, 17, and 18, on the return home of his body.[1] In these early drafts, Tennyson has already developed the stanza he was to adopt for the whole poem, a tetrameter quatrain, rhymed ABBA. There are some examples of this stanza in earlier poetry, but *In Memoriam* is by far the longest and best-known poem to use it; as a result the stanza is now commonly known as the *In Memoriam* stanza. It is an unusual choice for a long poem: the symmetrical eight-syllable line is far more apt to become monotonous than the longer ten-syllable one of iambic pentameter that from the sixteenth to the twentieth centuries was the norm for long English poems on elevated topics. Alongside the poem's confessional intimacy it also has the aspect of a formal exercise repeated over and over again; both kinds of writing can be strategies for coping with loss. The *In Memoriam* stanza makes forward progress difficult: the novelist Henry James wrote of the poem's style as a "poised and stationary" one, in which "the phrase always seems to me to pause and slowly pivot upon itself, or at most to move backwards."[2] This quality is partly an effect of the poem's rhyme scheme: while the couplet in English poetry usually produces closure, here it comes in the middle of the stanza, giving an appearance of closure from which, at the end of every stanza, the final rhyme draws us back to the beginning.

This stanza form is appropriate for a poetic sequence whose main formal principle is to plot the linear development of its speaker's feelings on the cyclical calendar of the recurring seasons and dates of the year. In the process of the poem's composition, this principle seems to have been in place by 1838, when Tennyson had composed two (sections 30 and 78) of the Christmas poems that help establish the time scheme of the finished sequence.

---

1   In the following chronology of *In Memoriam*'s composition, I have drawn upon the authoritative account in Susan Shatto and Marion Shaw's variorum edition (Oxford: Oxford UP, 1982).

2   Qtd in Christopher Ricks, *Tennyson* (New York: Macmillan, 1972), 228.

As *In Memoriam* grew, its concern with natural history and cosmology emerged in the late 1830s and the first half of the 1840s. During this time Tennyson broadened the scope of his work to consider not only the meaning of the death of individuals, but that of the extinction of species. Natural historians had begun to recognize extinctions as part of the history of life on earth since the late eighteenth century; by Tennyson's time there was wide agreement that the fossil record showed many former species that had no living representatives. This was the view of the great taxonomist Georges Cuvier, whose work *The Animal Kingdom* (1817) included both extant and extinct species in a single set of classifications. Charles Lyell, the leading geologist of the early nineteenth century, also accepted the evidence of past extinctions in his *Elements of Geology* (1830–34), which Tennyson read in the 1830s. Lyell's work popularized the idea of an old earth, in which geological features we see today have been shaped by the continuous slow operation of natural forces, a view that superseded the older view of a much shorter geological history, punctuated by cataclysms such as the biblical flood. The idea of a world where over time mountain ranges have been lifted up and carried away by erosion, where coastlines shift, and where continents can slowly subside and sink beneath the sea was Lyell's contribution to nineteenth-century thought, and it shaped the view of history that appears in Tennyson's poem. As well as displacing biblical history, this view of a continuously changing world also called into question the natural theology of the late eighteenth century, in which living creatures were viewed as endowed by God with the perfect design for their particular habitat and conditions of existence. The most influential writer in this tradition, William Paley, was required reading at Cambridge when Tennyson studied there; late in the composition of *In Memoriam* he added stanzas to section 124 explicitly rejecting Paley's argument that the perfection of natural structures such as the eye is evidence of providential design: "I found Him not in world or sun, / Or eagle's wing or insect's eye" (5–6).[1]

In Memoriam's concern with the death of a single individual thus broadens out to confront the challenge of a universe in which nothing stands outside history and whose changing elements reveal no divine plan. Part of the poem's solution to this challenge is the typically Victorian belief that in the long run,

---

1   See Appendix B, p. 157, for excerpts from works of theology, natural history, and philosophy that provide context for *In Memoriam*.

change is progress. For Tennyson, this belief leads to acceptance not only of species extinction, but also of a form of evolution. Though Darwin began working on the theory of natural selection in 1838, he was not to publish *The Origin of Species* until 1859, nine years after *In Memoriam*, and the idea of evolution that the poem adopts in its later sections differs fundamentally from that which Darwin was to propose, above all in viewing it as a process in which "lower" forms progress to "higher" and human beings lose their kinship with "brute" animals. When Tennyson wrote, species were generally regarded by both scientific and religious authorities as unchanging; nonetheless, a progressive conception of species evolution came to be widely accepted during the Victorian era, perhaps more so than Darwin's theory of evolution by means of natural selection.[1] Tennyson's view of evolution, along with that of many other members of the Victorian reading public, was influenced by the book *Vestiges of Creation*, anonymously published in 1844. The author was a Scottish publisher and journalist named Robert Chambers, and he proposed a progressive theory of divinely planned species evolution. Notwithstanding hostility from both the scientific and the religious establishments, the book was an immediate best-seller, far more so than *The Origin of Species* was to be.[2] Tennyson ordered a copy shortly after it appeared, and it influenced *In Memoriam*'s treatment of the progressive evolution of species.

Though the ideas explored in *In Memoriam* do not represent religious or scientific orthodoxy in the Victorian period, there was little in them to shock the general reader. Neither religious nor scientific ideas are presented in the poem in a conclusive way; it is not a philosophical work, and its religion does not take the form of dogmatic belief but of ritual practice. The poem performs a sequence of addresses, sometimes in the mode of prayer, sometimes of confession; sometimes these addresses constitute or commemorate an observance shared with others. Very often, they recollect or reinterpret other utterances from earlier in the series. The work of weaving these addresses together in time is the poem's meaning: it makes patterns in a temporal fabric and aims to reestablish what Hallam's early death, and more generally the

---

1 On Victorian ideas of progressive evolution, see Peter J. Bowler, *The Invention of Progress: The Victorians and the Past* (Oxford: Blackwell, 1989).

2 On *Vestiges*'s cultural impact see James A. Secord, *Victorian Sensation: The Extraordinary Publication, Reception, and Secret Authorship of Vestiges of the Natural History of Creation* (Chicago: U of Chicago P, 2000).

nineteenth century's cosmological revolution, had brought into question: the very idea that events have a proper time.

Genre, Form, and Structure

In Memoriam belongs to the period of literary history when the cultural authority of poetry first felt competition from the ascendant genre of the novel, with which it still shared a broad general readership. In terms of sales, both genres had benefited from the technological and social changes in the first half of the nineteenth century that exponentially increased both the size of the reading public and the number of printed books and periodicals available to it. In Tennyson's lifetime, sales of literary works had increased from the then-phenomenal 10,000 copies on the day of publication and 25,000 within the year achieved by Byron's *The Corsair* in 1814, to the 13,000 copies of *Rob Roy* Walter Scott sold in four editions during 1818, when the Waverley Novels were at the height of their success, to the 100,000 copies achieved by the parts of Dickens's *The Old Curiosity Shop* as it was published in serial form during 1840–41. In this context, the 8,000 copies of *In Memoriam*'s first four editions, all published in 1850,[1] amount to a relatively modest sale. Nonetheless, novels were at this date still widely viewed as popular entertainment, and they received little serious critical attention. *In Memoriam* by contrast received extensive reviews that discussed its formal achievements, its relation to the poetic tradition, the theological ideas it expressed, and its representation of male love and friendship.[2]

Tennyson certainly hoped for the kind of serious attention his poem in fact received. In conversation later in life he would describe the poem as a "kind of *Divina Commedia*" and assert that its speaker was "not always the author speaking of himself, but the voice of the human race speaking thro' him."[3] Besides Dante, reviewers compared the poet to Petrarch, Milton, Wordsworth, Shelley, and above all to the Shakespeare of the *Sonnets*, and we will return later to discussion of *In Memoriam*'s

---

1   For print runs of Byron and Scott, see William St. Clair, *The Reading Nation in the Romantic Period* (Cambridge: Cambridge UP, 2004), Appendix 9. For Dickens's sales, see Richard Altick, *The English Common Reader* (Chicago: U of Chicago P, 1957), Appendix B. For the sales of *In Memoriam*, see June Steffensen Hagen, *Tennyson and His Publishers* (University Park: Pennsylvania State UP, 1979), 84–85.

2   See Appendix E (p. 193) for selections from the reviews of *In Memoriam*.

3   See Appendix F (p. 203) for Tennyson's comments on the poem.

relation to the long histories of the love poem and the elegy. The poem's sales, though, are the result of its appeal to a broad middle-class readership, including both men and women, whose other reading would have consisted largely of prose. Like other poetry of the mid-nineteenth century, *In Memoriam* is thus set in a world recognizable to the novel reader, of realistically represented scenes of middle-class life. In Tennyson's poem, families put up Christmas decorations in the winter and enjoy picnics in the summer. They mourn in the parlor, while the household servants gather in the kitchen. Students at university hold parties in their rooms, and young men leave their friends in the country and travel to the metropolis to train for the professions. The poem commemorates holiday travel in remembering the trips Tennyson and Arthur Hallam took together to the Rhine and the south of France; it describes the Tennyson family moving away from the home in which the poet and his ten siblings had grown up. Unlike other major English elegies such as Milton's "Lycidas" (1637), Shelley's "Adonais" (1822), or Swinburne's "Ave Atque Vale" (1868), *In Memoriam* does not represent any supernatural beings or otherworldly settings. Like Dante's *Paradiso*, it ends with a wedding, but one that takes place in an English parish church and is followed by a reception with champagne and dancing on the rectory lawn.

In Memoriam is thus a more personal poem, more closely linked to the historical and social circumstances in which it was written, than earlier poetic elegies. It names Hallam—"my lost Arthur" (9, 3)—rather than transforming him into a mythical figure like Lycidas, Thyrsis, or Adonais. Though the poem does briefly adopt the conventions of pastoral elegy by representing its characters as shepherds (see sections 21–23), more usually the figures it represents or addresses as interlocutors are realistically represented Victorian men and women. Though Hallam is the only person actually named in the poem, it includes references to many real people we can identify, who would have been known to at least some of the poem's first readers: these include the poet's brother Charles, addressed in section 79, his friend the scholar Edmund Lushington, addressed in the final section, and the poet's sister Cecilia, whose wedding to Lushington the last section celebrates. These real characters coexist with others who have no original in Tennyson's life, but who are equally recognizable as belonging to the historical time and place in which the poem was written and set; these figures include for instance the bereaved characters of section 6: a father whose soldier son has died in battle abroad, a mother whose son has died at sea, and a young girl whose lover has fallen from his horse and died on his way to visit her.

In its representations of both real and fictional characters, then, the poem takes pains to establish its connection to mid-nineteenth-century history. In this period, England was a global military and economic power, whose soldiers and sailors worked and died abroad. It was a country undergoing the throes of a painful, uneven, and contested process of democratization, to which Tennyson refers in section 113. Elsewhere he contrasts what he celebrates as the gradual character of change in England to the three revolutionary overthrows of the constitution experienced by France in 1789, 1830, and 1848, which are mentioned in section 127. These facts of world history are not directly Tennyson's theme in *In Memoriam*, but the poem makes evident throughout the ways they have shaped the characters and situations it represents. For this reason, for all the poem's density of personal allusion, we should not think of its significance as limited to Tennyson and his circle; rather we should understand the poem as aiming to produce a set of representations that its readers would understand as historically and socially *typical*. By the end of the poem, Hallam himself appears as a "type"; the term derives from the Greek *tupos*, meaning stamp or impression, so that a type literally bears the stamp of a particular history or setting.

In Memoriam thus confines its action to the everyday world, and stresses the typical character of the events it relates. This is even, or especially, true of the event of death. Hallam's death itself appears early in the poem as "common" (section 6). As the sequence unfolds, the speaker observes the death-day's recurrent anniversaries, and on the third of them recognizes that the day itself is an ordinary day: for others it marks a birthday or a wedding anniversary. And even in experiencing the day as marked by Hallam's death, the speaker recognizes that he is one of a fellowship of others whose bereavement occurred on the same date, a fellowship brought into being by the contingent impression of tragic but everyday events.

The very ordinariness of the speaker's life is one of *In Memoriam*'s themes, and the poem mostly breaks with the Romantic convention of representing the poet as consecrated or endowed with special prophetic powers. Nonetheless, as the sequence unfolds, it tests the reality of all its own representations, and the appearance of ordinariness itself can become a source of error. Near the sequence's beginning, the speaker imagines the arrival in England of the ship returning Hallam's body for burial, and its passengers "stepping lightly down the plank, / And beckoning unto those they know" (14, 7–8). He goes on to imagine how Hallam himself on debarking would "strike a sudden hand in mine, / And ask a thousand things of home" (14, 11–12), and then console the friend whom his own death has bereaved. The everyday character of the scene of travelers arriving and greeting their friends masks the contradiction in its representation of Hallam as at once alive and dead; of this spectral, impossible encounter he has imagined, the poet ends the section by saying, "I should not feel it to be strange" (14, 20). Only late in the sequence is the speaker able to recognize the paradoxical strangeness of how familiar his dead friend is to him, and to address him now as "Strange friend, past, present, and to be" (129, 9).

The relation between the historically and socially determinate scenes of everyday life that make up *In Memoriam* is one of the poem's main topics. As we can see from the end of section 129, by the conclusion of the sequence the speaker understands different times as conjoined in one—past, present, and future all in the moment of a single address. The relation of different moments in time, staged in the poem as the problem of the relation between its component lyric sections, is announced as a problem at the very outset, when the speaker recalls that before he was bereaved, he had thought of his life as one in which he left behind his past as a series of "dead selves," turned to stone and serving as steps leading "to higher things" (1, 4). He announces that he has abandoned this idea, and will now cling to his grief, rather than leaving it behind him—a position that leads to the speaker's self-figuration in section 2 as the yew that clings to the bones of the dead. These opening sections introduce the topic of the relation of present to past, and provide the reader with training in seeing how this topic is embodied in the poem's form as a sequence of lyrics, each dramatizing a single moment of reflection or emotion. To read the poem is to find a way that leads from one section of the poem to the next. As the sequence develops, moreover, the moments dramatized in the sequence's component lyrics become more complex, and its representation of the lyric present becomes increasingly multifold.

One way the poem establishes relations between its individual lyric sections is by incorporating in them references to a framing calendar. Calendar poems whose different parts represent the changing seasons of the year have a long history that in English includes James Thompson's *The Seasons* (1726–30) and Edmund Spenser's *The Shepherd's Calendar* (1579), an adaptation of Virgilian pastoral eclogue. Another version of this tradition is the sequence of poems organized by the church calendar: the most influential Victorian example of this kind of calendar poem, a model for *In Memoriam*, was John Keble's sequence *The Christian Year* (1827), from which excerpts appear in Appendix D1 of this edition (p. 179). The main internal calendar of *In Memoriam* connects the sections by framing them as parts of a three-year narrative of mourning, in which the natural phenomena of the seasons appear in their proper order, as do secular and religious holidays such as New Year's Eve and Christmas. Besides the legal, religious, and natural calendars, the poem also marks the recurrence of dates that refer specifically to Hallam: his birthday (section 107) and the date of his death (sections 72 and 99). In representing a world where people and events bear the impress of history, *In Memoriam* shows that history is not monolithic: the poem's characters are affected by social and political history, but also by weather, and by the particularities of their own individual histories and those of their families and friends. For the middle class of Tennyson's time, as of ours, the sacred, natural, and legal calendars are supplemented by a cycle of private observances and recollections that make one of the rhythms of domestic life.

The series of lyric moments making up the individual sections of *In Memoriam* are thus arrayed in different calendars, some linear, some cyclical, that are, as it were, superimposed upon one another. Calendars themselves are artifacts that bear history's impress: as we've seen, the poem marks the arrival of the legal new year in January (section 106); it also, however, greets the new year in the spring (sections 83, 116), recalling both literary convention and the historical memory of the old legal calendar, in force until 1751, in which the new year began on 25 March. Moreover, of course, the three-year calendar of mourning that structures the poem's numbered sections is a fiction; as we know, almost seventeen years elapsed between Tennyson's composition of its earliest fragmentary parts and its eventual publication. During that time, he said, the "way of its being written was so queer that if there were a blank space I would put in a poem."[1] The calendar with its blank spaces is

---

1 Tennyson is quoted in James Knowles, "Aspects of Tennyson II (A Personal Reminiscence)," *Nineteenth Century* 33 (1893): 182.

the poem's organizing fiction, but its fictional status is announced within the poem itself by references in the framing sections to the actual time of writing. In every edition, the poem has a dedication—usually between the unnumbered opening section and section 1—with the date of Hallam's death: "In memoriam A. H. H. obiit MDCCCXXXIII." The opening section itself is dated 1849 after the last line. The poem is thus framed by references to a long chronology that coexists with its internal representation of a three-year mourning process. This long chronology returns in the wedding poem that concludes the sequence, which refers to the "thrice three years" since Hallam's death (10).

In Memoriam is thus a sequence of lyrics whose relation to one another is structured not just by one calendar, but by several. To read it is to step from one lyric "now" to another, while recognizing that each of these moments belongs to multiple chronologies, and occupies time in more than one way. Time moves at different speeds in the poem, so that the moment of an utterance can be defined by a season, as in section 115, "Now fades the last long streak of snow" (1), or by the incalculably long periods of time represented in section 123:

> The hills are shadows, and they flow
> From form to form, and nothing stands;
> They melt like mist, the solid lands,
> Like clouds they shape themselves and go.
>
> (5–9)

The mourning process in *In Memoriam* thus involves registering the passage of time by dating the events the poem relates and the recurrence of their anniversaries. In so doing, though, the poem refers to multiple calendars with different scales, and the result is that its very historical specificity leads to a sense of the superimposition of different times on one another at its key moments. This quality in *In Memoriam* arises in part from its use of the Christian mode of historical and scriptural interpretation known as typology. In a classic article on typological interpretation, Erich Auerbach cites two passages from St. Paul that he terms the "basis" of typology. These are 1 Cor. 10:6 and 11 "where the Jews in the desert are termed *typoi hemon* ('figures of ourselves'), and where it is written that 'these things befell them as figures (*typicos*)."[1] In these verses Paul establishes the schema for a mode of figural interpretation that became "one of the essential elements of the Christian picture of reality, history, and the concrete world in general."[2] In this schema, "figural interpretation establishes a connection between two events or persons, the first of which signifies not only itself but also the second, while the second encompasses or fulfills the first. The two poles of the figure are separate in time, but both, being real events ..., are within time, within the stream of historical life."[3] The crucial points here are that the type exists in historical time and that it links distinct events as instances of a single pattern.

The typological structure of *In Memoriam* is largely internal to the poem; in its simplest form it appears whenever an event from early in the poem is echoed by a later one, as in the poem's representation of three successive Christmases (sections 30, 78, 105) or of the speaker's two visits in sections 7 and 119 to Hallam's home in Wimpole Street. Strictly speaking, though, a type foreshadows a later event that both fulfills and supersedes it, as in St. Paul's view in which Jewish history is at once fulfilled and superseded by Christianity. The type offers a view of the truth that will in time be superseded. It is in the strong sense of the term that Tennyson uses "type" in section 33, displacing the temporal scale from the historical to the biographical. Here the term is associated with femininity and youth: a young girl believes in a literal idea of Heaven and attaches her faith to "flesh and blood" (11); her older brother has given up this kind of belief for a faith that does not "fix itself to form" (4). The poem asks the brother whether his faith is weaker than hers because it is not linked to a "type." This poem belongs with others in the sequence that link an attachment to the material body with femininity and childhood. Throughout the first

---

1 Erich Auerbach, "Figura," in *Scenes from the Drama of European Literature* (Minneapolis: U of Minnesota P; reprint, 1984), 49. The major treatments of Victorian typology are George P. Landow, *Victorian Types, Victorian Shadows: Biblical Typology in Victorian Literature, Art, and Thought* (Boston: Routledge & Kegan Paul, 1980) and Herbert L. Sussman, *Fact into Figure: Typology in Carlyle, Ruskin, and the Pre-Raphaelite Brotherhood* (Columbus: Ohio State UP, 1979). For an important discussion of language, natural history and the type in *In Memoriam*, see Isobel Armstrong, *Victorian Poetry: Poetry, Poetics, and Politics* (London and New York: Routledge, 1993), 247–63.

2 Auerbach, 33.

3 Auerbach, 53.

half of the poem the speaker's preoccupations with the body of his dead friend and with the idea of physical resurrection, as in the case of Lazarus, tend to feminize and infantilize him.

One way to read the poem is as dramatizing the speaker's progressive abandonment of the early sections' fixation on material things, in favor of a recognition of the strange, spiritual form of his friend's immortality. In keeping with the idea that attachment to material things is feminine and childish, the poem represents the speaker's development as growth to manhood. This reading explains the speaker's appearance in the poem's last section at a wedding where he performs a father's task of giving away the bride. But we have seen that the poem's calendar is not merely linear, but loops back on itself and superimposes different times upon one another, making it impossible to read the poem purely as a narrative of development. The last section, after all, is only one possible point of closure for the poem. *In Memoriam* opens, we have seen, with an unnumbered prologue dated 1849. The date tells us that it views the whole poem in retrospect, including the final section; and its retrospective description of the poem characterizes it entirely as the "Confusions of a wasted youth" (42). The first section is thus also a kind of close for the poem, and one that undermines the apparent serenity of the last.

The poem's typological structure gives it a view of time in which nothing is ever fully superseded. Rather, the relation between types and their fulfillment remains the subject of continuous contestation and debate, as in section 33. And, though the term "type" originally entered the English language in the theological sense discussed above, by the nineteenth century the term's meaning had enormously extended. In *In Memoriam* Tennyson uses it in its then-recent taxonomical sense to refer to biological species, and, especially in sections 55–56, to examine how, like the theological type, these are subject to history. Typology in its traditional sense also developed to consider not only, as in St. Paul, the historical relation of Judaism to Christianity, but the relation between successive historical forms of religious belief more generally. These are superimposed onto one another in section 121, where a typological view of history provides the frame for Tennyson's reflections on his poem's structure and meaning and on the relation between the speaker's past and present. In this five-stanza section, the first two are set in the evening, after sunset; the second two at dawn, before sunrise. The present moment in each pair of stanzas is established by one of *In Memoriam*'s most characteristic rhetorical devices, the figure of direct address or apostrophe, where the address to a person or thing establishes its presence in a poem's dramatic situation. Here, the first two stanzas of the poem are addressed to Hesper, in Greek mythology the personification of the evening star, while the second two are addressed to Phosphor, personifying the star of morning. The former appears as a mourner, grieving "o'er the buried sun, / And ready, thou, to die with him" (1–2); the latter is defined by her anticipation of the day to come. The argument of the section depends on the astronomical knowledge that these two personifications are different names for the same planet, Venus, which can be seen only in the evening or morning; the mourner of the first pair of stanzas and the day-bringer of the second are thus one and the same: "Thou, like my present and my past, / Thy place is changed; thou art the same" (19–20).

The section's interpretation thus depends at once on two kinds of knowledge, belonging to different historical moments: knowledge of the Greek pantheon and its personifications of celestial bodies, and knowledge of elementary astronomy. To these we should add a third: the planet Venus's name comes from the Latin name of the goddess of love, one of the archetypal mourners of the elegiac tradition, whose grief over the dead Adonis is an explicit topos in the genre from its beginning in Moschus's "Lament for Bion" up to Shelley's "Adonais" and is an implicit point of reference for the series of female mourners in Tennyson's own poem.[1] The poem's meaning thus superimposes three different cosmologies on one another, in a moment that does not itself have any specifiable historical place. The last stanza makes this point in the context of the individual life of the speaker: "Sweet Hesper-Phosphor, double name / For what is one, the first, the last, / Thou, like my present and my past, / Thy place is changed; thou art the same" (17–20). If the time of the section's first four stanzas was defined by the addresses they make to Hesper in the evening and Phospor in the morning, a stanza addressed to both Hesper and Phosphor combines two times in one. This joining of past and present occurs in a moment outside linear time, as the stanza implies by its reference to the end of time in the Book of Revelation: "I am the Alpha and the Omega, the beginning and the end, the first and the last" (22.13). Auerbach writes that this apocalyptic perspective is always

---

1 On the female mourner in male elegy see Peter M. Sacks, *The English Elegy: Studies in the Genre from Spenser to Yeats* (Baltimore: Johns Hopkins UP, 1985). Sacks's chapter on *In Memoriam* is the fullest treatment of the poem's typological structure.

implicit in typological reading, which interprets "one worldly event through another; the first signifies the second, the second fulfills the first. Both remain historical events; yet both ... have something provisional or incomplete about them; they point to one another and both point to something in the future ... which will be the actual, real, and definitive event.... Thus history, with all its concrete force, remains forever a figure, cloaked and needful of interpretation."[1] The typological view of history as concrete, but also in need of interpretation with reference to an extra-historical, apocalyptic time is *In Memoriam*'s most important structuring principle.

Elegy, Sonnet Sequence, and Sexuality

Like all of Tennyson's long poems, *In Memoriam* is a generic hybrid. We have already discussed the poem's relation to eclogue and other kinds of calendar poetry; most basically, though, as a poem whose central topics are mourning and the search for consolation after a friend's death, *In Memoriam* is an elegy. Mourning the dead is one of poetry's most ancient functions; as a literary tradition elegy begins in Greece with Theocritus' first *Idyll* (third century BCE), Bion of Smyrna's "Lament for Adonis," and Moschus' "Lament for Bion" (second century BCE). All three poems are rooted in archaic myths and fertility rituals: they are set in pastoral societies organized around animal herding, and they all mourn young men whose deaths ultimately find compensation in the annual cycle that brings newborn animals and the return of plant life in the spring. The poems all to some extent suppose an identification between the poets and the youths they mourn; often they are both shepherds, or both poets, or both. On the other hand, the dead youth is also in every case set apart from other young men by exceptional gifts and by the early death that these gifts somehow cause. Bion's "Lament for Adonis" takes its theme directly from the legend of Adonis, who was beloved of Venus and killed by a wound in the groin from a wild boar; the death of Adonis, as well as those of other figures associated with fertility cults such as Daphnis and Hylas, are regularly invoked by analogy elsewhere in the tradition.

The goddess who mourns the dead youth but is also to blame for having failed to save him remains a central figure in elegy throughout its history. Her presence poses a problem for the Christianized version of the genre developed by John Milton in

1   Auerbach, 58.

"Lycidas," where she is present in the form of the muse Calliope, who cannot save her son Orpheus from death and dismemberment at the hands of women devotees of Dionysus. For Milton, narratives of mourning and consolation involving pagan goddesses appear in the elegy only to be dismissed as the expression of "false surmise" (53) regarding Lycidas' fate, which is in fact to be "mounted high" in Heaven through Christian grace.

In Memoriam is undoubtedly an elegy; in sections 21–23 it even adopts the conventions of the pastoral to represent Tennyson and Hallam in their days at Cambridge under the guise of shepherds in Arcadia. From the elegiac tradition comes the prominence of female mourners in Tennyson's poem; the converse tradition of blaming women for a young man's death is also reflected in the deadly appearance of Nature in sections 55 and 56. The Miltonic representation of the wrong kind of grief as an emasculating seduction of the male mourner informs the representation of Sorrow as a seductress in section 3 of *In Memoriam*.

Notwithstanding Tennyson's adoption of these aspects of elegy's traditional sexual plot, *In Memoriam* remains an anomaly in the genre. As we have seen, elegy from the beginning represents the gods as involved in human life and death: they bear responsibility, they participate in the process of mourning, and they provide consolation. Even in post-classical elegy, though the pagan deities are represented only as fictions, Christ can be a source of consolation, or poetry itself can be given a divinizing power. Milton represents Lycidas as like a star "mounted high, / Through the dear might of him that walked the waves" (172–73), and even in "Adonais" (1822), Shelley's radically skeptical elegy for his fellow poet Keats, Adonais appears at the poem's close beckoning "like a star ... from the abode where the Eternal are" (494–95). In Tennyson's poem the dead friend's transformation into a star at the close is reversed: the last section imagines the conception of a child and pictures how "a soul"—perhaps Hallam's—"shall draw from out the vast / And strike his being into bounds" (123–24), moving in the opposite direction from Adonais and Lycidas, from the heavens to earth.

This reversal suggests how thoroughly *In Memoriam*'s attention is fixed on the human world. Even the seasonal cycle, whose centrality in Tennyson's poem is one of its points of connection to the long tradition of elegy, does not provide consolation; in the poem's internal calendar, the mourning process does not follow the seasons but rather extends as we have seen over a multi-year calendar. The poem's very length makes it unique among elegies;

historically poems in the genre include a dramatic turn from grief to consolation, often motivated by an encounter with the divine. Milton has: "Weep no more, woeful shepherds, weep no more, / For Lycidas your sorrow is not dead" (165–66), and Shelley: "Peace, peace! He is not dead, he doth not sleep— / He hath awakened from the dream of life" (343–44). *In Memoriam* offers no such once-and-for-all breakthrough; everything that happens in the poem is repeated, qualified, and reinterpreted, and the poem's work of self-reading and interpretation is a major part of its action. The nearest it comes to the traditional elegiac turn is section 95. The main action of this section is rereading: alone at night, the speaker rereads Hallam's letters and experiences a moment of communion:

> So word by word, and line by line,
>> The dead man touch'd me from the past,
>> And all at once it seem'd at last
> The living soul was flash'd on mine,
>
> And mine in this was wound, and whirl'd
>> About empyreal heights of thought,
>> And came on that which is, and caught
> The deep pulsations of the world.
>
> (33–40)

Following this, though, the speaker's own experience becomes a text: "At length my trance / Was cancell'd, stricken thro' with doubt" (43–44). These lines figure the speaker's trance as a passage in a text under revision: it becomes a cancel, a passage stricken through or crossed out to be marked for deletion. The passage echoes the poem's description of Hallam's death itself in section 72 as an event in which a "dark hand struck down through time, / And cancelled nature's best" (19–20). In this view, the poem's movement is not from separation to reunion, or from error to truth, but rather from a partial to a fuller reading, one that ultimately encompasses even passages that have been crossed out or marked as doubtful.

The recurrent idea in *In Memoriam* that records of the past are incomplete and require interpretation to be made whole is particularly apt because, besides elegy, the poem's other major generic affiliation is with sequences of love poems, a genre whose nineteenth-century history was decisively influenced by editorial work in the late eighteenth century. The only edition of Shakespeare's *Sonnets* to appear in his lifetime was published in 1609; it has been the basis of every subsequent text. In 1640 a publisher named George Benson published a pirated edition, which combined sonnets into longer poems, altered the 1609 order, combined Shakespeare's work with that of other poets, and in some of the sonnets changed male pronouns to female. The resultant text dominated the market, such as it was, for Shakespeare's lyric poetry until the end of the eighteenth century, when in 1780 Edmond Malone produced a new edition that restored the order and wording of 1609. One result was the reemergence of the sonnet sequence, and ultimately of lyric sequences more generally, as a major nineteenth-century genre. Charlotte Smith's *Elegiac Sonnets* (1784) and William Lisle Bowles's *Fourteen Sonnets* (1789) were both best-selling sonnet sequences published in the wake of Malone's edition. With respect to Shakespeare, Malone's publication had two related effects: it made it possible to read the *Sonnets* as a confessional narrative in which Shakespeare represents himself in the first person, and it set them at the center of the debate that surrounded the nineteenth century's construction of the figure of the male homosexual as a criminal and pathological case. Malone's edition set the stage for the sequence's divided reception; his notes defend it against—while also rehearsing—charges of indecency.[1] Throughout the nineteenth century, anxiety about the possibility that Shakespeare was a sodomite alternated with praise of the *Sonnets* as portraying an ennobling male friendship.

The *Sonnets*'s contested nineteenth-century reception is a vital part of the context for *In Memoriam*. In writing a deeply personal poem that relates the development of his own feelings and character through the medium of a sequence of lyrics, Tennyson adopts the prevailing contemporary reading of Shakespeare's sequence as a model for his own portrayal of love between men. He undoubtedly did so in full awareness of the division of opinion about the *Sonnets*; Arthur Hallam admired them, but after his death his father Henry disparaged them in his *Introduction to the Literature of Europe in the 15th, 16th, and 17th Centuries* (1839):

---

1   On Malone's edition and its reception, see Peter Stallybrass "Editing as Cultural Formation: The Sexing of Shakespeare's Sonnets," *MLQ* 54.1 (1993): 91–103. Rpt *Shakespeare's Sonnets: Critical Essays*, James Schiffer, ed. (New York: Garland, 1993), 75–88.

These sonnets were long overlooked; Steevens spoke of them with the utmost scorn, as productions which no one could read; but a very different suffrage is generally given by the lovers of poetry, and perhaps there is now a tendency, especially among young men of poetical tempers, to exaggerate the beauties of these remarkable productions.... Notwithstanding the frequent beauties of these sonnets, ... it is impossible not to wish that Shakspeare had never written them. There is a weakness and folly in all excessive and misplaced affection, which is not redeemed by the touches of nobler sentiments that abound in this long series of sonnets.[1]

Tennyson more than once told friends of his own disagreement with this judgment: the *Memoir* records him saying of the *Sonnets*, "Henry Hallam made a great mistake about them: they are noble."[2]

In taking the sonnet sequence as a model for his most personal poem, Tennyson makes the same choice as Elizabeth Barrett Browning in her *Sonnets from the Portuguese*, published like *In Memoriam* in 1850 (see Appendix D2, p. 184). The two poets established a renewed vogue for the sequence as a genre of love poetry, reflected in major works over the next two decades by Coventry Patmore, Christina Rossetti, George Meredith, Dante Rossetti, and Augusta Webster, among others. On its publication, the affinity between *In Memoriam* and the *Sonnets* was widely noted in the reviews (see the selection in Appendix E, p. 193), and the nineteenth century's split judgment of Shakespeare's sequence was to some extent reproduced in the reception of Tennyson's. Writing in *Fraser's Magazine* in September 1850 Charles Kingsley rejoiced to find from *In Memoriam* "that the heart of man still beats young and fresh; that the old tales of David and Jonathan, Damon and Pythias, Socrates and Alcibiades, Shakespeare and his nameless friend, of 'love passing the love of woman,' ennobled by its own humility, deeper than death, and mightier than the grave, can still blossom out"; the following year, however, a reviewer in *The Times* took the opposite view, complaining of the poem's "tone of—may we say so?—amatory tenderness" and asking, "very sweet and plaintive these verses are; but who would not give them a feminine application? Shak-

---

1   Henry Hallam, *Introduction to the Literature of Europe in the 15th, 16th, and 17th Centuries* (Paris: Galignani, 1839), 3: 289–91.

2   Hallam Tennyson, *Alfred, Lord Tennyson: A Memoir by his Son* (London: Macmillan, 1897), 2: 289.

speare may be considered the founder of this style in English. In Classical and Oriental poetry it is unpleasantly familiar. His mysterious sonnets present the startling peculiarity of transferring every epithet of womanly endearment to a masculine friend,—his master-mistress, as he calls him by a compound epithet, harsh as it is disagreeable."

The Times's review is unusual in its distaste for *In Memoriam*, and there is no evidence that the poem was caught up in the homosexual panic that became a central feature of British masculine identity in the latter part of the century. As Alan Sinfield has shown, though, Tennyson was responsive to changes in the social policing of male friendship after the poem was published, as was his son when he revised the *Memoir* to omit Benjamin Jowett's reference to Tennyson's love of Shakespeare's *Sonnets* as "a sort of sympathy with Hellenism."[1] Criticism in the twentieth and twenty-first centuries remains divided about whether the poem challenges the heteronormative culture of its time: Sinfield writing in 1986 saw the poem's confusion of gender categories as "risky"; since then, however, Jeff Nunokawa has argued that it tells a thoroughly normative story that associates queer desire with boyhood, making it only a stage on the path to adult masculinity, while Sarah Rose Cole has criticized the very idea that there was any contradiction between male friendships and heterosexual marriage in early Victorian society, noting that the friendship formed between Hallam and Tennyson at university led to the engagement of Hallam and Tennyson's sister Emily.[2]

Mourning and Marriage

Tennyson's friendship with Hallam led not only to the latter's engagement, but also to his own. His protracted courtship of another Emily, Emily Sellwood, began when Hallam introduced them, two days after recognizing his own attachment to Emily Tennyson. Robert Martin writes in his biography about the similarity of the two love affairs—not least in the identity of the two women's names—and concludes "that Alfred was unconsciously

---

1 Alan Sinfield, *Alfred Tennyson* (Oxford: Blackwell 1986), 128.
2 Sinfield, 136; Jeff Nunokawa, "*In Memoriam* and the Extinction of the Homosexual," *ELH* 58 (1991): 427–38; Sarah Rose Cole, "The Recovery of Friendship: Male Love and Developmental Narrative in *In Memoriam*." *Victorian Poetry* 50.1 (2012): 43–66.

imitating what happened to his friend."[1] Alfred and Emily had a brief engagement in the late 1830s but broke it off in 1840, partly because Alfred could not afford to marry and partly because of Emily's doubts about his religious beliefs. *In Memoriam* brought about the renewal of their engagement; in late 1849 Alfred wrote to Emily for the first time since the breach, and he had a friend give her a copy of the as-yet untitled elegies in March of 1850. After reading them, she accepted his renewed proposal; the eventual title *In Memoriam* was her suggestion. The poem was published on 1 June 1850, and less than two weeks later, on the 13th, the couple was married. They spent their honeymoon in the Lake District; on their way they stopped at Clevedon, Somerset where they visited Hallam's grave. During the elegies' composition Tennyson had not been there; to visit now, they thought, "seemed a kind of consecration" of their marriage.[2]

Alfred and Emily's marriage is thus doubly mediated by Hallam: in falling in love with his wife, Tennyson takes his friend as a model, and in renewing his courtship, he offers the elegies for Hallam as a gift. Though this narrative can be read to show how male friendship in Victorian culture functioned to advance the heterosexual marriage plot, it can also be read to show the opposite. The part of *In Memoriam* that seems most directly offered as a gift to Emily Sellwood is the opening section, with its dating in 1849, the year of their reconciliation. And as we have seen, this section's relation to the sequence as a whole is that of a retraction that begs forgiveness for the speaker's waste of his youth. On this reading, Tennyson's love for Hallam functions not as a means to his eventual marriage, but as an obstacle to be overcome. Tennyson's work on *In Memoriam*, the work of mourning Hallam, had to be brought to a close before his marriage could take place.[3]

It is not necessary to choose between these readings; *In Memoriam* is a great poem because it expresses one man's love for another in a society and at a historical moment when the meaning of love between men was changing and radically uncertain. More generally, the poem argues that love survives death—and it does so at a time when old ideas about the immortality of

---

1   Robert Bernard Martin, *Tennyson: The Unquiet Heart* (Oxford: Oxford UP, 1980), 104.

2   Hallam Tennyson, *Memoir* 1: 332.

3   This paragraph summarizes ideas from Matthew Rowlinson, "The Thing in the Poem: *Maud*'s Hymen," *differences* 12.3 (2001): 128–65.

poetic ideas on the one hand, and of the body on the other, had lost some purchase but still retained their power to challenge newer biopolitical ideas of survival through sexual reproduction of the race or species. *In Memoriam* was published in 1850, at the beginning of the decade when spiritualism and the practice of communion with the dead through mediums became a transatlantic vogue.[1] The later part of the nineteenth century saw the revival of Gothic fiction and the emergence of neo-Paganism in authors such as Swinburne, Pater, and Kipling—both literary developments that produce eroticized representations of the resurrected dead. *In Memoriam* anticipates these developments, as it does the cult of mourning that settled over the monarchy after Victoria's husband, Prince Albert, died in 1861. The poem's centrality for its period, and its importance for ours, thus arise from its addressing and working-through of the most conflicted topics in the intimate life of Victorian society.

---

1   For a work of fiction that connects *In Memoriam* and spiritualism, see A.S. Byatt's novella "The Conjugial Angel" in *Angels and Insects* (London: Chatto and Windus, 1992).

Alfred Tennyson: A Brief Chronology

[This chronology is based on F.B. Pinion's *A Tennyson Chronology* (Houndmills, Hampshire: Macmillan, 1990) and on the chronology in Christopher Ricks's *The Poems of Tennyson*.]

1809   Alfred Tennyson (AT) born on 6 August, the fourth child of Rev. George Clayton Tennyson, Rector of Somersby, Lincolnshire, and his wife Elizabeth. Alfred and his 10 surviving brothers and sisters grew up together at Somersby, where the family lived until 1837.

1811   Birth of Arthur Henry Hallam (AHH).

1815–20   AT attends Louth Grammar School; except for these five years he was educated at home by his father.

1823–24   Writes a verse drama, *The Devil and the Lady*.

1827   In April AT anonymously publishes *Poems by Two Brothers*, including his work and that of his older brothers Charles and Frederick. In November he joins Charles and Frederick as a student at Trinity College, Cambridge.

1828   AHH enters Trinity in October.

1829   Beginning of friendship between AT and AHH. In May they are elected to the "Apostles," an undergraduate literary society. In June, AT wins the Chancellor's Gold Medal for poetry, for which he and AHH had both submitted entries. AHH makes his first visit to Somersby in December, and meets Emily Tennyson.

1830   In April AHH visits Somersby again and begins his courtship of Emily. In May, at his father's wish, he withdraws from a joint volume of poems planned with AT. AT publishes *Poems, Chiefly Lyrical* in June as a solo volume, the arrangements having been made by AHH. Between July and September AT and AHH travel in France, meeting in the Pyrenees with Spanish Constitutionalist guerillas, to whom they deliver mail and funds from Britain. In December, back in Cambridge, demonstrations in support of the Reform Bill threaten the university. Students including AT and AHH patrol with the constabulary.

AT and other students assist in putting out a fire set by arsonists at nearby Coton.

1831 On 16 March AT's father George dies after many years of alcoholism. AT leaves Cambridge without a degree; his uncle urges him to enter the Church. In August AHH publishes "On Some Characteristics of Modern Poetry and on the Lyrical Poems of Alfred Tennyson" in *Englishman's Magazine*.

1832 AHH graduates from Cambridge in January. On June 7 the Reform Bill passes, after three years of political crisis. The electorate is enlarged from about 400,000 to about 650,000 men; the franchise is limited by a property qualification. In July AHH and AT visit the Rhine country. In December AT publishes a new volume, *Poems*.

1833 AHH's engagement to Emily Tennyson is recognized by the Hallam family. AHH studies law in London. In August he leaves for a trip to eastern Europe with his father, after visiting Emily in Somersby. On 15 September AHH dies in his hotel room in Vienna. The Tennyson family receives the news in a letter from AHH's uncle at the beginning of October. On 6 October AT composes what was to be sect. 9 of *In Memoriam*, "Fair ship, that from the Italian shore." During the succeeding fall he writes "Ulysses," "Tithon," and other poems—some of which were to find a place in *In Memoriam*—and begins work on "Morte d'Arthur."

1834 AHH buried in Clevedon Church. His father publishes *Remains in Verse and Prose of Arthur Henry Hallam* and gives Emily Tennyson an annual allowance of £300, as he had agreed to do on her planned marriage to AHH.

1837 In May the Tennysons move from Somersby to High Beech, Epping. In June William IV dies and is succeeded on the throne by his 18-year old niece Victoria.

1838 AT engaged to Emily Sellwood.

1840 The engagement is broken off partly because of AT's financial insecurity and partly because of Emily's doubts about his religious orthodoxy.

1840–41 AT stays as a guest at an asylum for the insane. The proprietor, Matthew Allen, promotes a scheme to make wood-carvings by machinery, in which AT

	invests his fortune (about £3000). By 1843 the business has collapsed and AT loses everything but an insurance policy on Allen's life.
1842	In May AT publishes *Poems*. The collection is in two volumes; the first includes revised versions of poems from the volumes of 1830 and 1832 and the second consists of new work.
1843	AT takes the water cure at a hospital near Cheltenham.
1845	He is granted a government pension of £200 a year.
1847	In December AT publishes *The Princess*.
1848	Revolution across Europe and in Latin America. In France Louis Philippe is forced from the monarchy and a republic is declared.
1849	AT and Emily Sellwood renew correspondence.
1850	On 1 June AT publishes *In Memoriam*. On 13 June he and Emily Sellwood are married. On their wedding-trip, they visit AHH's grave. In November AT is appointed Poet Laureate, succeeding William Wordsworth, who had died in April.
1852	Publishes "Ode on the Death of the Duke of Wellington."
1855	*Maud, and Other Poems.*
1859	*Idylls of the King*, namely "Enid," "Vivien," "Elaine," and "Guinevere."
1864	*Enoch Arden, and Other Poems.*
1865	Refuses the offer of a baronetcy; the offer was repeated with the same result in 1873 and 1874.
1869	*The Holy Grail and Other Poems.*
1872	Publishes *Gareth and Lynette, Etc.* With the exception of "Balin and Balan," written in 1874, this volume completes the *Idylls of the King*, which appear together in a new edition of the *Works*.
1880	*Ballads and Other Poems.*
1883	Accepts the offer of a barony and assumes the title Lord Tennyson.
1885	*Tiresias and Other Poems.*
1886	*Locksley Hall Sixty Years After, Etc.*
1889	*Demeter and Other Poems.*
1892	AT dies 6 October. The burial takes place in Westminster Abbey on 12 October. On 28 October his final volume, *The Death of Oenone, Akbar's Dream, and Other Poems* appears.

A Note on the Text

The text of this edition is that of the Eversley Edition (1907–08), edited by the poet's son Hallam. Eversley includes all revisions Tennyson made to the poem between its first publication and his death in 1892, and this edition follows its wording exactly. In a few passages where its capitalization or punctuation differ from those of the editions printed in the poet's lifetime, these have been adopted from earlier editions. Eversley also includes annotation by Tennyson himself and by his son, and many of these notes are reproduced here. Notes by Tennyson himself are marked with his initial: (T).

Besides the authorial notes in Eversley, we have a source for Tennyson's own ideas about *In Memoriam* in a transcript made by James Knowles of his running comments on it. Knowles published some of this commentary in "Aspects of Tennyson II: A Personal Reminiscence" (*Nineteenth Century* 33 [1893]: 164–88); his manuscript notes were printed in Gordon Ray's *Tennyson Reads Maud* (Vancouver: Publications Centre, U of British Columbia, 1968). Footnotes to this edition include selected authorial commentary from both sources. In keeping with the aim of making the poem accessible for teaching and study, the notes gloss unfamiliar words and difficult passages. They explain allusions, particularly to other English poems, and list some important manuscript and printed variants. For a full record of textual variants, readers should consult the variorum edition by Susan Shatto and Marion Shaw. Both Shatto and Shaw's edition and that of Christopher Ricks give fuller listings of sources and analogous passages than I have attempted here.

IN MEMORIAM.

LONDON:
EDWARD MOXON, DOVER STREET.
1850.

Title page of *In Memoriam*'s first edition. Courtesy University of Toronto libraries.

IN MEMORIAM A.H.H.

OBIIT MDCCCXXXIII.[1]

Strong Son of God, immortal Love,[2]
    Whom we, that have not seen thy face,
    By faith, and faith alone, embrace,
Believing where we cannot prove;

Thine are these orbs[3] of light and shade;   5
    Thou madest Life in man and brute;
    Thou madest Death; and lo, thy foot
Is on the skull which thou hast made.

Thou wilt not leave us in the dust:
    Thou madest man, he knows not why,   10
    He thinks he was not made to die;
And thou hast made him: thou art just.

Thou seemest human and divine,
    The highest, holiest manhood, thou:
    Our wills are ours, we know not how;   15
Our wills are ours, to make them thine.

Our little systems have their day;
    They have their day and cease to be:
    They are but broken lights of thee,
And thou, O Lord, art more than they.   20

We have but faith: we cannot know;
    For knowledge is of things we see;

---

1 The Latin means, "In memory of A.H.H., died 1833." In every single-volume edition of the poem Tennyson published, this formula appeared as a dedication between the unnumbered opening section and section 1, though the Eversley Edition moved it to its position here. The single-volume editions all give the title on a separate page as *In Memoriam*, without identifying either the poem's subject or its author.

2 "This might be taken in a St. John sense" (T). Hallam Tennyson adds a reference to 1 John chapters 4 and 5.

3 "Sun and moon" (T). "Orbs" can also refer to eyes, as in *Paradise Lost* 3.25.

And yet we trust it comes from thee,
A beam in darkness: let it grow.

Let knowledge grow from more to more,   25
    But more of reverence in us dwell;
    That mind and soul, according well,
May make one music as before,[1]

But vaster. We are fools and slight;
    We mock thee when we do not fear: 30
    But help thy foolish ones to bear;
Help thy vain worlds to bear thy light.

Forgive what seemed my sin in me;
    What seemed my worth since I began;
    For merit lives from man to man,   35
And not from man, O Lord, to thee.

Forgive my grief for one removed,
    Thy creature, whom I found so fair.
    I trust he lives in thee, and there
I find him worthier to be loved.   40

Forgive these wild and wandering cries,
    Confusions of a wasted youth;
    Forgive them where they fail in truth,
And in thy wisdom make me wise.

                                        1849.[2]

---

1 "As in the ages of faith" (T).
2 The unnumbered opening section is the only one to which Tennyson
   appended a date. The date 1849 establishes that this section views the
   sequence in retrospect, though it appears at the beginning. The section
   belongs to the genre of the poetic retraction, in which the poet reviews
   his own work and begs forgiveness for its failures.

I.

I held it truth, with him who sings
    To one clear harp in divers tones,
    That men may rise on stepping-stones
Of their dead selves to higher things.[1]

But who shall so forecast the years   5
    And find in loss a gain to match?
    Or reach a hand thro' time to catch
The far-off interest of tears?

Let Love clasp Grief lest both be drown'd,[2]
    Let darkness keep her raven gloss: 10
    Ah, sweeter to be drunk with loss,
To dance with death, to beat the ground,

Than that the victor Hours should scorn
    The long result of love, and boast,
    "Behold the man that loved and lost,   15
But all he was is overworn."[3]

II.

Old Yew,[4] which graspest at the stones
    That name the under-lying dead,
    Thy fibers net the dreamless head,
Thy roots are wrapt about the bones.

---

1 Tennyson identifies "him" in line 1 as the German writer Goethe, and
   adds, "Among his last words were: ... from changes to higher changes."
   Hallam Tennyson adds: "My father would often say, 'Goethe is consum-
   mate in so many different styles.'" We know from the title that the
   sequence is an elegy, but it begins with the speaker's relation not to his
   dead friend but to his dead self.
2 "Love" and "Grief" are personifications of the speaker's own feelings,
   holding on to each other and keeping each other alive. These are the
   first of the poem's images of clasping and grasping.
3 Shakespeare, *Sonnets* 63: 1–2: "my love shall be as I am now / With
   Time's injurious hand crush'd and o'erworn."
4 The yew tree, evergreen and long-lived, is often found in British grave-
   yards. Here its changelessness and its grip on the dead make it a double
   for the speaker who addresses it. This section is also *about* the literary
   figures of address and doubling: the yew is also a "you," into which the
   speaker becomes "incorporate."

The seasons bring the flower again,   5
    And bring the firstling to the flock;
    And in the dusk of thee, the clock
Beats out the little lives of men.

O not for thee the glow, the bloom,
    Who changest not in any gale,   10
    Nor branding summer suns avail
To touch thy thousand years of gloom:

And gazing on thee, sullen tree,
    Sick for thy stubborn hardihood,
    I seem to fail from out my blood   15
And grow incorporate into thee.

III.
O Sorrow, cruel fellowship,
    O Priestess in the vaults of Death,
    O sweet and bitter in a breath,
What whispers from thy lying lip?[1]

"The stars," she whispers, "blindly run;   5
    A web is wov'n across the sky;
    From out waste places comes a cry,
And murmurs from the dying sun:

"And all the phantom, Nature, stands—
    With all the music in her tone,   10
    A hollow echo of my own,—
A hollow form with empty hands."

And shall I take a thing so blind,
    Embrace her as my natural good;
    Or crush her, like a vice of blood,[2]   15
Upon the threshold of the mind?[3]

---

1   "Sorrow" is another personification of the speaker's feelings. She in
    turn refers to a phantom, "Nature," as her double and echo.
2 *Othello* 1.3.123: "I do confess the vices of my blood."
3 The speaker asks if he should marry his sorrow or kill her.

IV.

To Sleep I give my powers away;
    My will is bondsman to the dark;
    I sit within a helmless bark,[1]
And with my heart I muse and say:

O heart, how fares it with thee now,   5
    That thou shoulds't fail from thy desire,
    Who scarcely darest to inquire,
"What is it makes me beat so low?"

Something it is which thou hast lost,
    Some pleasure from thine early years.   10
    Break, thou deep vase of chilling tears,
That grief hath shaken into frost![2]

Such clouds of nameless trouble cross
    All night below the darken'd eyes;
    With morning wakes the will, and cries,   15
"Thou shalt not be the fool of loss."

V.

I sometimes hold it half a sin
    To put in words the grief I feel;
    For words, like Nature, half reveal
And half conceal the Soul within.

But, for the unquiet heart and brain,   5
    A use in measured language lies;
    The sad mechanic exercise,
Like dull narcotics, numbing pain.

In words, like weeds,[3] I'll wrap me o'er,
    Like coarsest clothes against the cold: 10

---

1 In this first of a series of poems about ships, the vessel without a helm is
   an image of the speaker, whose mind in sleep is not governed by his
   will. The image derives from courtly love poetry; compare Thomas
   Wyatt's "My galley charged with forgetfulness."

2 "Water can be brought below freezing-point and not turn into ice—if it
   be kept still; but if it be moved suddenly it turns into ice and may break
   the vase" (T).

3 "Weeds" are mourning clothes, usually a widow's.

But that large grief which these enfold
Is given in outline and no more.[1]

VI.

One writes, that "Other friends remain,"
    That "Loss is common to the race"—
    And common is the commonplace,
And vacant chaff well meant for grain.

That loss is common would not make   5
    My own less bitter, rather more:
    Too common![2] Never morning wore
To evening, but some heart did break.

O father, wheresoe'er thou be,
    Who pledgest now thy gallant son;
    A shot, ere half thy draught be done,   10
Hath still'd the life that beat from thee.

O mother, praying God will save
    Thy sailor,—while thy head is bow'd,
    His heavy-shotted hammock-shroud   15
Drops in his vast and wandering grave.

Ye know no more than I who wrought
    At that last hour to please him well;[3]
    Who mused on all I had to tell,
And something written, something thought;   20

Expecting still his advent home;
    And ever met him on his way
    With wishes, thinking, "here to-day,"
Or "here to-morrow will he come."

O somewhere, meek, unconscious dove,   25
    That sittest ranging golden hair;

---

1 Compare *Hamlet* 1.2.85–86: "But I have that within which passes show, / These but the trappings and the suits of woe."
2 *Hamlet* 1.2.72: "Thou know'st 'tis common, all that lives must die."
3 Hallam Tennyson notes, "my father was writing to Arthur Hallam in the hour that he died."

And glad to find thyself so fair,
Poor child, that waitest for thy love![1]

For now her father's chimney glows
    In expectation of a guest;   30
    And thinking "this will please him best,"
She takes a riband or a rose;

For he will see them on to-night;
    And with the thought her colour burns
    And, having left the glass, she turns   35
Once more to set a ringlet right;

And, even when she turn'd, the curse
    Had fallen, and her future Lord
    Was drown'd in passing thro' the ford,
Or kill'd in falling from his horse.   40

O what to her shall be the end?
    And what to me remains of good?
    To her, perpetual maidenhood,
And unto me no second friend

VII.

Dark house, by which once more I stand
    Here in the long unlovely street,[2]
    Doors, where my heart was used to beat
So quickly, waiting for a hand,

A hand that can be clasp'd no more—   5
    Behold me, for I cannot sleep,

---

1 The "meek, unconscious dove" preparing for the arrival of a lover who
    is already dead, like the father and mother earlier in the section, is a
    generic figure whose ignorance of her own loss provides an image for
    that of the speaker. In inventing her, Tennyson may have thought of his
    sister Emily, Arthur Hallam's fiancée, though Emily's hair was dark, not
    "golden." Emily did not in fact accept perpetual maidenhood, marrying
    Richard Jesse in 1842.
2 "67 Wimpole Street" (T), the house of Arthur Hallam's father Henry.
    On the affinities between this section and the genre of Greek and
    Roman love poem in which an excluded lover addresses the door that
    separates him from his mistress, see Shatto and Shaw 169.

And like a guilty thing I creep
At earliest morning to the door.[1]

He is not here; but far away[2]
    The noise of life begins again,   10
    And ghastly thro' the drizzling rain
On the bald street breaks the blank day.

VIII.

A happy lover who has come
    To look on her that loves him well,
    Who 'lights and rings the gateway bell,
And learns her gone and far from home;

He saddens, all the magic light   5
    Dies off at once from bower and hall,
    And all the place is dark, and all
The chambers emptied of delight:

So find I every pleasant spot
    In which we two were wont to meet,   10
    The field, the chamber and the street,
For all is dark where thou art not.

Yet as that other, wandering there
    In those deserted walks, may find
    A flower beat with rain and wind,   15
Which once she foster'd up with care;

So seems it in my deep regret,
    O my forsaken heart, with thee
    And this poor flower of poesy
Which little cared for fades not yet.   20

But since it pleased a vanish'd eye,
    I go to plant it on his tomb,

---

1 In *Hamlet* 1.1.148 old Hamlet's ghost starts "like a guilty thing" when
    summoned back to Purgatory by the arrival of morning. Wordsworth's
    "Ode: Intimations of Immortality" echoes Shakespeare: "tremble like a
    guilty thing surprised" (149).
2 Luke 24.6: "He is not here, but is risen."

That if it can it there may bloom,
Or dying, there at least may die.[1]

IX.[2]

Fair ship, that from the Italian shore
    Sailest the placid ocean-plains
    With my lost Arthur's loved remains,[3]
Spread thy full wings, and waft him o'er.

So draw him home to those that mourn   5
    In vain; a favourable speed
    Ruffle thy mirror'd mast, and lead
Thro' prosperous floods his holy urn.

All night no ruder air perplex
    Thy sliding keel, till Phosphor,[4] bright   10
    As our pure love, thro' early light
Shall glimmer on the dewy decks.

Sphere all your lights around, above;
    Sleep, gentle heavens, before the prow;
    Sleep, gentle winds, as he sleeps now,   15
My friend, the brother of my love;

My Arthur whom I shall not see
    Till all my widow'd race be run;
    Dear as the mother to the son,
More than my brothers are to me.   20

X.

I hear the noise about thy keel;
    I hear the bell struck in the night:
    I see the cabin-window bright;
I see the sailor at the wheel.

---

1 With this image of the poem as a flower, compare *Sonnets from the Por-*
    tuguese 44 in Appendix D2, p. 186.
2 Section 9 was written on 6 October 1833; it was the first-written section
    of the poem. Sections 17 and 18 were written shortly after. The subse-
    quent addition of sections 10–16 produced a sequence of 10 sections,
    each of 5 stanzas, on the return of Hallam's body to England.
3 The first mention of Hallam by name.
4 "Star of dawn" (T). The planet Venus when it appears in the morning.

Thou bring'st the sailor to his wife,   5
    And travell'd men from foreign lands;
    And letters unto trembling hands;
And, thy dark freight, a vanish'd life.

So bring him: we have idle dreams:
    This look of quiet flatters thus   10
    Our home-bred fancies: O to us,
The fools of habit, sweeter seems

To rest beneath the clover sod,
    That takes the sunshine and the rains,
    Or where the kneeling hamlet drains   15
The chalice of the grapes of God;

Than if with thee the roaring wells
    Should gulf him fathom-deep in brine;
    And hands so often clasp'd in mine,
Should toss with tangle[1] and with shells.[2]   20

XI.

Calm is the morn without a sound,
    Calm as to suit a calmer grief,
    And only thro' the faded leaf
The chestnut pattering to the ground:

Calm and deep peace on this high wold,   5
    And on these dews that drench the furze,
    And all the silvery gossamers
That twinkle into green and gold:

Calm and still light on yon great plain
    That sweeps with all its autumn bowers,   10
    And crowded farms and lessening towers,
To mingle with the bounding main:

---

1 "Oar-weed (*laminaria digitata*)" (T).
2 Compare Ovid, *Tristia* 1.2.52–54: "demite naufragium, mors mihi
   munerus erit. / est aliquid, fatove suo ferrove cadentem / in solida
   moriens ponere corpus humo" (Save me from shipwreck and death will
   be a boon. 'Tis something worth if falling by fate or by the steel one
   rests in death upon the solid ground). See also Milton, "Lycidas"
   152–58.

Calm and deep peace in this wide air,
    These leaves that redden to the fall;
    And in my heart, if calm at all,   15
If any calm, a calm despair:

Calm on the seas, and silver sleep,
    And waves that sway themselves in rest,
    And dead calm in that noble breast
Which heaves but with the heaving deep.   20

XII.

Lo, as a dove when up she springs
    To bear thro' Heaven a tale of woe,[1]
    Some dolorous message knit below
The wild pulsation of her wings;[2]

Like her I go; I cannot stay;   5
    I leave this mortal ark behind,
    A weight of nerves without a mind,
And leave the cliffs, and haste away

O'er ocean-mirrors rounded large,
    And reach the glow of southern skies,   10
    And see the sails at distance rise,
And linger weeping at the marge,

And saying; "Comes he thus, my friend?
    Is this the end of all my care?"
    And circle moaning in the air: 15
"Is this the end? Is this the end?"

And forward dart again, and play
    About the prow, and back return
    To where the body sits and learn
That I have been an hour away.   20

---

1 Genesis 8.8–9: "Also he sent forth a dove from him, to see if the waters
   were abated from off the face of the ground; but the dove found no rest
   for the sole of her foot, and she returned unto him in the ark."
2 The speaker compares himself to a carrier pigeon.

XIII.

Tears of the widower, when he sees
    A late-lost form that sleep reveals,
    And moves his doubtful arms, and feels
Her place is empty, fall like these;[1]

Which weep a loss for ever new,   5
    A void where heart on heart reposed;
    And, where warm hands have prest and closed,
Silence, till I be silent too.

Which weep the comrade of my choice,
    An awful thought, a life removed,   10
    The human-hearted man I loved,
A Spirit, not a breathing voice.

Come Time, and teach me, many years,
    I do not suffer in a dream;
    For now so strange do these things seem,   15
Mine eyes have leisure for their tears;

My fancies time to rise on wing,
    And glance about the approaching sails,
    As tho' they brought but merchants' bales,
And not the burthen that they bring.   20

XIV.

If one should bring me this report,
    That thou hadst touch'd the land to-day,[2]
    And I went down unto the quay,
And found thee lying in the port;

And standing, muffled round with woe,   5
    Should see thy passengers in rank
    Come stepping lightly down the plank,
And beckoning unto those they know;

And if along with these should come
    The man I held as half-divine;   10

---

1 Compare Milton, Sonnet 19, "Methought I saw my late espoused saint."
2 Like sections 9, 10, 15, and 17, section 14 is addressed to the ship car-
    rying Hallam's body.

Should strike a sudden hand in mine,
And ask a thousand things of home;

And I should tell him all my pain,
      And how my life had droop'd of late,
      And he should sorrow o'er my state   15
And marvel what possess'd my brain;

And I perceived no touch of change,
      No hint of death in all his frame,
      But found him all in all the same,
I should not feel it to be strange.   20

                        XV.
To-night the winds begin to rise
      And roar from yonder dropping day:
      The last red leaf is whirl'd away,[1]
The rooks are blown about the skies;

The forest crack'd, the waters curl'd,   5
      The cattle huddled on the lea;
      And wildly dash'd on tower and tree
The sunbeam strikes along the world:

And but for fancies, which aver
      That all thy motions gently pass   10
      Athwart a plane of molten glass,
I scarce could brook the strain and stir

That makes the barren branches loud;
      And but for fear it is not so,
      The wild unrest that lives in woe   15
Would dote and pore on yonder cloud

That rises upward always higher,
      And onward drags a labouring breast,
      And topples round the dreary west,
A looming bastion fringed with fire.   20

---

1   Coleridge, "Christabel" 49–50: "The one red leaf, the last of its clan, /
    That dances as often as dance it can."

XVI

What words are these have fall'n from me?
    Can calm despair and wild unrest
    Be tenants of a single breast,
Or sorrow such a changeling be?

Or doth she only seem to take   5
    The touch of change in calm or storm;
    But knows no more of transient form
In her deep self, than some dead lake

That holds the shadow of a lark
    Hung in the shadow of a heaven?   10
    Or has the shock, so harshly given,
Confused me like the unhappy bark

That strikes by night a craggy shelf,
    And staggers blindly ere she sink?
    And stunn'd me from my power to think   15
And all my knowledge of myself;

And made me that delirious man
    Whose fancy fuses old and new,
    And flashes into false and true,
And mingles all without a plan?   20

XVII

Thou comest, much wept for: such a breeze
    Compell'd thy canvas, and my prayer
    Was as the whisper of an air
To breathe thee over lonely seas.

For I in spirit saw thee move   5
    Thro' circles of the bounding sky,
    Week after week: the days go by:
Come quick, thou bringest all I love.

Henceforth, wherever thou may'st roam,
    My blessing, like a line of light,   10
    Is on the waters day and night,
And like a beacon guards thee home.

So may whatever tempest mars
    Mid-ocean, spare thee, sacred bark;
    And balmy drops in summer dark   15
Slide from the bosom of the stars.

So kind an office hath been done,
    Such precious relics brought by thee;
    The dust of him I shall not see
Till all my widow'd race be run.[1]   20

XVIII.

'Tis well; 'tis something; we may stand
    Where he in English earth is laid,
    And from his ashes may be made
The violet of his native land.[2]

'Tis little; but it looks in truth   5
    As if the quiet bones were blest
    Among familiar names to rest
And in the places of his youth.

Come then, pure hands, and bear the head
    That sleeps or wears the mask of sleep,   10
    And come, whatever loves to weep,
And hear the ritual of the dead.

Ah yet, ev'n yet, if this might be,
    I, falling on his faithful heart,
    Would breathing thro' his lips impart   15
The life that almost dies in me;

That dies not, but endures with pain,
    And slowly forms the firmer mind,
    Treasuring the look it cannot find,
The words that are not heard again.   20

---

1 On human life as a race, see 1 Corinthians 9.24–27.
2 Tennyson cites *Hamlet* 5.1.238–40: "Lay her i' th' earth, / And from her
    fair and unpolluted flesh / May violets spring!"

XIX.[1]

The Danube to the Severn gave[2]
  The darken'd heart that beat no more;
  They laid him by the pleasant shore,
And in the hearing of the wave.

There twice a day the Severn fills;   5
  The salt sea-water passes by,
  And hushes half the babbling Wye,
And makes a silence in the hills.[3]

The Wye is hush'd nor moved along,
  And hush'd my deepest grief of all, 10
  When fill'd with tears that cannot fall,
I brim with sorrow drowning song.

The tide flows down, the wave again
  Is vocal in its wooded walls;
  My deeper anguish also falls, 15
And I can speak a little then.

XX.

The lesser griefs that may be said,
  That breathe a thousand tender vows,
  Are but as servants in a house
Where lies the master newly dead;

Who speak their feeling as it is,   5
  And weep the fulness from the mind:
  "It will be hard," they say, "to find
Another service such as this."

My light moods are like to these,
  That out of words a comfort win; 10
  But there are other griefs within,
And tears that at their fountain freeze;

---

1 According to Hallam Tennyson, this section was written at Tintern Abbey.

2 "He died at Vienna and was brought to Clevedon to be buried" (T).

3 "Taken from my own observation—the rapids of the Wye are stilled by the incoming sea" (T).

For by the hearth the children sit
    Cold in that atmosphere of Death,
    And scarce endure to draw the breath,   15
Or like to noiseless phantoms flit:

But open converse is there none,
    So much the vital spirits sink
    To see the vacant chair, and think,
"How good! how kind! And he is gone."   20

XXI.

I sing to him that rests below,
    And, since the grasses round me wave,
    I take the grasses of the grave,
And make them pipes whereon to blow.[1]

The traveller hears me now and then,   5
    And sometimes harshly will he speak:
    "This fellow would make weakness weak,
And melt the waxen hearts of men."

Another answers, "Let him be,
    He loves to make parade of pain   10
    That with his piping he may gain
The praise that comes to constancy."

A third is wroth: "Is this an hour
    For private sorrow's barren song,
    When more and more the people throng   15
The chairs and thrones of civil power?[2]

"A time to sicken and to swoon,
    When Science reaches forth her arms

---

1   The figure of the poet as a piper is a pastoral convention, and this
    section is the first of a series in the genre of pastoral elegy.
2   Compare sections 127 and 128. Britain experienced Chartist demon-
    strations for the extension of the franchise throughout the period of *In
    Memoriam*'s composition. In France, the revolution of July 1830 brought
    about the overthrow of the last Bourbon king and the establishment of a
    constitutional monarchy. Revolution broke out again in 1832 and 1848;
    the latter year saw the establishment of the short-lived Second Republic.

   To feel from world to world, and charms
Her secret from the latest moon?"[1]   20

Behold, ye speak an idle thing:
     Ye never knew the sacred dust:
     I do but sing because I must,
And pipe but as the linnets sing:

And one is glad; her note is gay,   25
     For now her little ones have ranged;
     And one is sad; her note is changed,
Because her brood is stol'n away.

XXII.

The path by which we twain did go,[2]
     Which led by tracts that pleased us well,
     Thro' four sweet years arose and fell,[3]
From flower to flower, from snow to snow:

And we with singing cheer'd the way,   5
     And, crown'd with all the season lent,
     From April on to April went,
And glad at heart from May to May:

But where the path we walk'd began
     To slant the fifth autumnal slope,   10
     As we descended following Hope,
There sat the Shadow fear'd of man;

Who broke our fair companionship,
     And spread his mantle dark and cold,
     And wrapt thee formless in the fold,   15
And dull'd the murmur on thy lip,

---

1 Possibly a reference to the discovery of the planet Neptune in 1846,
   which occurred after perturbations in the orbit of Uranus were observed
   in the previous decade.

2 The image of life as a journey introduced in this section implies a linear
   view of time, where things happen only once. This linear time contrasts
   with the cyclical time of the seasons, which dominates the two friends'
   experience during their four glad years.

3 The four years of Hallam and Tennyson's friendship; probably 1829–33.
   A manuscript version has "three" instead of "four," while section 46.12
   speaks of *five* years.

And bore thee where I could not see
    Nor follow, tho' I walk in haste,
    And think, that somewhere in the waste
The Shadow sits and waits for me.   20

XXIII.

Now, sometimes in my sorrow shut,
    Or breaking into song by fits,
    Alone, alone, to where he sits,
The Shadow cloak'd from head to foot,

Who keeps the keys of all the creeds,[1]   5
    I wander, often falling lame,
    And looking back to whence I came,
Or on to where the pathway leads;

And crying, How changed from where it ran
    Thro' lands where not a leaf was dumb;   10
    But all the lavish hills would hum
The murmur of a happy Pan:[2]

When each by turns was guide to each,
    And Fancy light from Fancy caught,
    And Thought leapt out to wed with Thought   15
Ere Thought could wed itself with Speech;

And all we met was fair and good,
    And all was good that Time could bring,
    And all the secret of the Spring
Moved in the chambers of the blood;   20

And many an old philosophy
    On Argive heights divinely sang,
    And round us all the thicket rang
To many a flute of Arcady.[3]

---

1 "After death we shall learn the truth of all beliefs" (T).

2 The goat-god Pan presides over Greek pastoral poetry.

3 "Argive" means "Greek"; the Greek district of Arcadia is a traditional
    setting of pastoral poetry.

XXIV.

And was the day of my delight
  As pure and perfect as I say?
  The very source and fount of Day
Is dash'd with wandering isles of night.[1]

If all was good and fair we met,   5
  This earth had been the Paradise
  It never look'd to human eyes
Since our first Sun arose and set.[2]

And is it that the haze of grief
  Makes former gladness loom so great?   10
  The lowness of the present state,
That sets the past in this relief?

Or that the past will always win
  A glory from its being far;
  And orb into the perfect star   15
We saw not, when we moved therein?

XXV.

I know that this was Life,—the track
  Whereon with equal feet we fared;
  And then, as now, the day prepared
The daily burden for the back.

But this it was that made me move   5
  As light as carrier-birds in air;
  I loved the weight I had to bear,
Because it needed help of Love:

Nor could I weary, heart or limb,
  When mighty Love would cleave in twain   10
  The lading of a single pain,
And part it, giving half to him.

---

1 "Sun-spots" (T).
2 From the first edition until 1875, line 8 read "Since Adam left his
  garden yet."

XXVI.

Still onward winds the dreary way;
    I with it; for I long to prove
    No lapse of moons can canker Love,
Whatever fickle tongues may say.

And if that eye which watches guilt   5
    And goodness, and hath power to see[1]
    Within the green the moulder'd tree,
And towers fall'n as soon as built—

Oh, if indeed that eye foresee
    Or see (in Him is no before)   10
    In more of life true life no more
And Love the indifference to be,

Then might I find, ere yet the morn
    Breaks hither over Indian seas,
    That Shadow waiting with the keys,   15
To shroud me from my proper scorn.

XXVII.

I envy not in any moods
    The captive void of noble rage,
    The linnet born within the cage,
That never knew the summer woods:

I envy not the beast that takes   5
    His license in the field of time,
    Unfetter'd by the sense of crime,
To whom a conscience never wakes;

Nor, what may count itself as blest,
    The heart that never plighted troth   10
    But stagnates in the weeds of sloth;
Nor any want-begotten rest.

I hold it true, whate'er befall;
    I feel it, when I sorrow most;

---

1 "The Eternal Now. I AM" (T).

'Tis better to have loved and lost   15
Than never to have loved at all.[1]

XXVIII.[2]

The time draws near the birth of Christ:
 The moon is hid; the night is still;
 The Christmas bells from hill to hill
Answer each other in the mist.

Four voices of four hamlets round,   5
 From far and near, on mead and moor,
 Swell out and fail, as if a door
Were shut between me and the sound:

Each voice four changes on the wind,
 That now dilate, and now decrease,   10
 Peace and goodwill, goodwill and peace,
Peace and goodwill, to all mankind.

This year I slept and woke with pain,
 I almost wish'd no more to wake,
 And that my hold on life would break   15
Before I heard those bells again:

But they my troubled spirit rule,
 For they controll'd me when a boy;
 They bring me sorrow touch'd with joy,
The merry merry bells of Yule.   20

---

1 Noting the echoes in this stanza of section 1, lines 1 and 15, A.C.
 Bradley says that here the poem comes to a break, "as though a definite
 stage of advance were reached" (107).

2 In the internal chronology of the poem, sections 28–30 refer to the
 Christmas following Hallam's death. They are set in Somersby rectory,
 where Tennyson grew up. Sections 28 and 29 describe Christmas Eve in
 the present tense; the time of section 30 is Christmas morning. Sections
 28 and 30 date from late 1833 or 1834 and are thus early in the poem's
 actual process of composition.

XXIX.

With such compelling cause to grieve
    As daily vexes household peace,
    And chains regret to his decease,
How dare we keep our Christmas-eve;

Which brings no more a welcome guest   5
    To enrich the threshold of the night
    With shower'd largess of delight
In dance and song and game and jest?

Yet go, and while the holly boughs
    Entwine the cold baptismal font,   10
    Make one wreath more for Use and Wont,
That guard the portals of the house;

Old sisters of a day gone by,
    Gray nurses, loving nothing new;
    Why should they miss their yearly due   15
Before their time? They too will die.

XXX.

With trembling fingers did we weave
    The holly round the Christmas hearth;
    A rainy cloud possess'd the earth,
And sadly fell our Christmas-eve.

At our old pastimes in the hall   5
    We gambol'd, making vain pretence
    Of gladness, with an awful sense
Of one mute Shadow watching all.

We paused: the winds were in the beech:
    We heard them sweep the winter land;   10
    And in a circle hand-in-hand
Sat silent, looking each at each.

Then echo-like our voices rang;
    We sung, tho' every eye was dim,
    A merry song we sang with him   15
Last year: impetuously we sang:

We ceased: a gentler feeling crept
    Upon us: surely rest is meet:
    "They rest," we said, "their sleep is sweet,"
And silence follow'd, and we wept.   20

Our voices took a higher range;
    Once more we sang: "They do not die
    Nor lose their mortal sympathy,
Nor change to us, although they change;

"Rapt from the fickle and the frail   25
    With gather'd power, yet the same,
    Pierces the keen seraphic flame
From orb to orb, from veil to veil."[1]

Rise, happy morn,[2] rise, holy morn,
    Draw forth the cheerful day from night: 30
    O Father, touch the east, and light
The light that shone when Hope was born.[3]

XXXI.

When Lazarus left his charnel-cave,
    And home to Mary's house return'd,
    Was this demanded—if he yearn'd
To hear her weeping by his grave?

"Where wert thou, brother, those four days?"   5
    There lives no record of reply,
    Which telling what it is to die
Had surely added praise to praise.

From every house the neighbours met,
    The streets were fill'd with joyful sound,   10
    A solemn gladness even crown'd
The purple brows of Olivet.

---

1 Shelley, "Adonais" 493–95: "Whilst burning through the inmost veil of
   Heaven, / The soul of Adonais, like a star, / Beacons from the abode
   where the Eternal are."
2 Milton, "On the Morning of Christ's Nativity" 1: "This is the month,
   and this the happy morn."
3 Hallam Tennyson notes, "My father often said: 'The cardinal point of
   Christianity is the life after death.'"

Behold a man raised up by Christ!
  The rest remaineth unreveal'd;
  He told it not; or something seal'd   15
The lips of that Evangelist.[1]

XXXII.

Her eyes are homes of silent prayer,
  Nor other thought her mind admits
  But, he was dead, and there he sits,
And he that brought him back is there.

Then one deep love doth supersede   5
  All other, when her ardent gaze
  Roves from the living brother's face,
And rests upon the Life indeed.[2]

All subtle thought, all curious fears,
  Borne down by gladness so complete,   10
  She bows, she bathes the Saviour's feet
With costly spikenard and with tears.[3]

Thrice blest whose lives are faithful prayers,
  Whose loves in higher love endure;
  What souls possess themselves so pure,   · 15
Or is there blessedness like theirs?

XXXIII.

O thou that after toil and storm
  Mayst seem to have reach'd a purer air,
  Whose faith has centre everywhere,
Nor cares to fix itself to form,

Leave thou thy sister when she prays,   5
  Her early Heaven,[4] her happy views;

---

1 The evangelist is St. John, whose Gospel tells the story of Jesus raising
  Lazarus from the dead after four days. Tennyson cites John 11.31, "she
  goeth unto the grave to weep there," said of Mary, Lazarus' sister.
2 John 11.25: "Jesus said unto her, I am the resurrection, and the life."
3 John 12.3: "Then took Mary a pound of ointment of spikenard, very
  costly, and anointed the feet of Jesus."
4 A.C. Bradley notes, "the Heaven of which she was taught in childhood"
  (113).

Nor thou with shadow'd hint confuse
A life that leads melodious days.

Her faith thro' form is pure as thine,
    Her hands are quicker unto good: 10
    Oh, sacred be the flesh and blood
To which she links a truth divine!

See thou, that countest reason ripe
    In holding by the law within,
    Thou fail not in a world of sin,   15
And ev'n for want of such a type.[1]

XXXIV.

My own dim life should teach me this,
    That life shall live for evermore,
    Else earth is darkness at the core,
And dust and ashes all that is;

This round of green, this orb of flame,   5
    Fantastic beauty; such as lurks
    In some wild Poet, when he works
Without a conscience or an aim.

What then were God to such as I?
    'Twere hardly worth my while to choose   10
    Of things all mortal, or to use
A little patience ere I die;

'Twere best at once to sink to peace,
    Like birds the charming serpent draws,
    To drop head-foremost in the jaws   15
Of vacant darkness and to cease.

---

1   The sister adheres to the forms of Christian belief, maintaining faith in
the flesh and blood of the historical Jesus as an example—or type—of
conduct. The section's addressee, presumably her brother, holds a faith
that is not attached to form, but only to reason and conscience—the law
within. *In Memoriam* vacillates between these positions; here it uses the
addressee and his sister as exemplary figures—types—to examine them.

XXXV.

Yet if some voice that man could trust
 Should murmur from the narrow house,
 "The cheeks drop in; the body bows;
Man dies: nor is there hope in dust:"

Might I not say? "Yet even here,   5
 But for one hour, O Love, I strive
 To keep so sweet a thing alive:"
But I should turn mine ears and hear

The moanings of the homeless sea,
 The sound of streams that swift or slow   10
 Draw down Æonian hills,[1] and sow
The dust of continents to be;[2]

And Love would answer with a sigh,
 "The sound of that forgetful shore[3]
 Will change my sweetness more and more,   15
Half-dead to know that I shall die."

O me, what profits it to put
 An idle case? If Death were seen
 At first as Death, Love had not been,
Or been in narrowest working shut,   20

Mere fellowship of sluggish moods,
 Or in his coarsest Satyr-shape
 Had bruised the herb and crush'd the grape,
And bask'd and batten'd in the woods.[4]

---

1   "The everlasting hills" (T).

2   See Appendix B2 (p. 160) for an excerpt from Charles Lyell's *Principles
  of Geology* describing "the immensity of time required for the annihila-
  tion of whole continents."

3   The "forgetful shore" is the shore that brings forgetfulness. Compare
  Milton's "forgetful lake" in *Paradise Lost* 2.74.

4   To "batten" is to feed. In *Hamlet* 3.4.67 and "Lycidas" 29 Shakespeare
  and Milton use it to describe grazing animals.

XXXVI.

Tho' truths in manhood darkly join,
    Deep-seated in our mystic frame,
    We yield all blessing to the name
Of Him that made them current coin;

For Wisdom dealt with mortal powers,   5
    Where truth in closest words shall fail,
    When truth embodied in a tale
Shall enter in at lowly doors.[1]

And so the Word had breath,[2] and wrought
    With human hands the creed of creeds   10
    In loveliness of perfect deeds,
More strong than all poetic thought;

Which he may read that binds the sheaf,
    Or builds the house, or digs the grave,
    And those wild eyes that watch the wave   15
In roarings round the coral reef.[3]

XXXVII.[4]

Urania[5] speaks with darken'd brow:
    "Thou pratest here where thou art least;
    This faith has many a purer priest,
And many an abler voice than thou

"Go down beside thy native rill,   5
    On thy Parnassus[6] set thy feet,
    And hear thy laurel whisper sweet
About the ledges of the hill."

---

1 "For divine Wisdom had to deal with the limited powers of humanity, to
    which truth logically argued out would be ineffectual, whereas truth
    coming in the story of the Gospel can influence the poorest" (T).
2 John 1.14: "and the Word was made flesh."
3 "By this is intended the Pacific Islanders, 'wild' having a sense of 'bar-
    barian' in it" (T).
4 "The Heavenly muse bids the poet's muse sing on a less lofty theme" (T).
5 Urania was traditionally the muse of astronomy, but Milton makes her
    the muse of sacred poetry in *Paradise Lost*—see 7.1–20.
6 Mountain sacred to Apollo and the muses.

And my Melpomene[1] replies,
     A touch of shame upon her cheek: 10
     "I am not worthy ev'n to speak
Of thy prevailing mysteries;

"For I am but an earthly Muse,
     And owning but a little art
     To lull with song an aching heart,   15
And render human love his dues;

"But brooding on the dear one dead,
     And all he said of things divine,
     (And dear to me as sacred wine
To dying lips is all he said),   20

"I murmur'd, as I came along,
     Of comfort clasp'd in truth reveal'd;
     And loiter'd in the master's field,[2]
And darken'd sanctities with song."

XXXVIII.

With weary steps I loiter on,
     Tho' always under alter'd skies
     The purple from the distance dies,
My prospect and horizon gone.

No joy the blowing[3] season gives,   5
     The herald melodies of spring,
     But in the songs I love to sing
A doubtful gleam of solace lives.

If any care for what is here
     Survive in spirits render'd free,   10
     Then are these songs I sing of thee
Not all ungrateful to thine ear.

---

1 The muse of tragedy and, as here, of elegy.
2 "The province of Christianity" (T).
3 "The blossoming season" (T). In the sequence's internal chronology,
   this section and the next mark the spring after Hallam's death.

XXXIX.[1]

Old warder of these buried bones,
    And answering now my random stroke
    With fruitful cloud and living smoke,[2]
Dark yew, that graspest at the stones

And dippest toward the dreamless head,   5
    To thee too comes the golden hour
    When flower is feeling after flower;
But Sorrow—fixt upon the dead,

And darkening the dark graves of men,—
    What whisper'd from her lying lips?   10
    Thy gloom is kindled at the tips,
And passes into gloom again.[3]

XL.[4]

Could we forget the widow'd hour
    And look on Spirits breathed away,
    As on a maiden in the day
When first she wears her orange-flower![5]

When crown'd with blessing she doth rise   5
    To take her latest leave of home,
    And hopes and light regrets that come
Make April of her tender eyes;

---

1 Published in 1870, this was the last-written section of *In Memoriam*; Tennyson added it to the poem as a pendant to Section 2.

2 "The yew, when flowering, in a wind or if struck sends up its pollen like smoke" (T). Ricks compares Lyell's *Principles of Geology* "How often, during the heat of a summer's day, do we see the males of dioecious plants, such as the yew-tree, standing separate from the females, and sending off into the air, upon the slightest breath of wind, clouds of buoyant pollen!" (2.55). A dioecious species has separate male and female plants.

3 These last two lines seem to be spoken by Sorrow, addressing the yew. Compare the reference to Sorrow's "lying lip" in section 3.

4 Tennyson said to James Knowles: "See Poem 97 where the writer is compared to the female—*here* the spirit becomes the female in the parable" (Ray 38).

5 Orange blossom is traditional at weddings. Queen Victoria wore an orange blossom wreath at her wedding in 1840.

And doubtful joys the father move,
    And tears are on the mother's face,   10
    As parting with a long embrace
She enters other realms of love;

Her office there to rear, to teach,
    Becoming as is meet and fit
    A link among the days, to knit   15
The generations each with each;

And, doubtless, unto thee is given
    A life that bears immortal fruit
    In those great offices that suit
The full-grown energies of heaven.   20

Ay me, the difference I discern!
    How often shall her old fireside
    Be cheer'd with tidings of the bride,
How often she herself return,

And tell them all they would have told,   25
    And bring her babe, and make her boast,
    Till even those that miss'd her most
Shall count new things as dear as old:

But thou and I have shaken hands,
    Till growing winters lay me low;   30
    My paths are in the fields I know,
And thine in undiscover'd lands.[1]

XLI.[2]

Thy spirit ere our fatal loss
    Did ever rise from high to higher;
    As mounts the heavenward altar-fire,
As flies the lighter thro' the gross.

---

1 "I have parted with thee until I die, and my paths are in the fields I
   know, whilst thine are in lands which I do not know" (T). Compare
   Shakespeare, Hamlet 3.1.78–79: "the undiscover'd country, from whose
   bourn / No traveller returns," and Shelley, "Alastor" 77: "To seek
   strange truths in undiscovered lands."

2 In sections 41–47 the poem speculates on death and the relation of life
   to the afterlife. The sections propose different views: of   (continued)

But thou art turn'd to something strange,[1]   5
    And I have lost the links that bound
    Thy changes; here upon the ground,
No more partaker of thy change.

Deep folly! yet that this could be—
    That I could wing my will with might   10
    To leap the grades of life and light,
And flash at once, my friend, to thee.

For tho' my nature rarely yields
    To that vague fear implied in death;
    Nor shudders at the gulfs beneath,   15
The howlings from forgotten fields;[2]

Yet oft when sundown skirts the moor
    An inner trouble I behold,
    A spectral doubt which makes me cold,
That I shall be thy mate no more,   20

Tho' following with an upward mind
    The wonders that have come to thee,
    Thro' all the secular to-be,[3]
But evermore a life behind.

---

death as a second birth into a new life; of death as sleep; of death as a
merging "in the general soul." Some sections, like 42, reject arguments
made in an earlier section; others, like 47, modify and qualify their own
arguments. The speculation ends with section 48, when the poem dis-
claims any idea of closing the questions it has opened, and 49, when it
characterizes itself as a pool, rippled on the surface by "random influ-
ences."

1 Shakespeare, *The Tempest* 1.2.402: "something rich and strange."
2 "The eternal miseries of the Inferno" (T). Hallam Tennyson refers to
    Dante's *Inferno* 3.25–51. See also Shakespeare *Measure for Measure*
    3.1.126–27: "those that lawless and incertain thought / Imagine
    howling" and *Hamlet* 5.1.241–42: "a minist'ring angel shall my sister be /
    When thou liest howling."
3 "Aeons of the future" (T).

XLII.

I vex my heart with fancies dim:
    He still outstript me in the race;[1]
    It was but unity of place
That made me dream I rank'd with him.

And so may Place retain us still,   5
    And he the much-beloved again,
    A lord of large experience, train
To riper growth the mind and will:

And what delights can equal those
    That stir the spirit's inner deeps,   10
    When one that loves but knows not, reaps
A truth from one that loves and knows?

XLIII.[2]

If Sleep and Death be truly one,
    And every spirit's folded bloom
    Thro' all its intervital gloom
In some long trance should slumber on;

Unconscious of the sliding hour,   5
    Bare of the body, might it last,

---

1 A continuation and correction of the previous section. The speaker rejects his fear that, having died first, Hallam will always be ahead of him: he was ahead in the race even when they were alive together.

2 Tennyson explains: "If the immediate life after death be only sleep, and the spirit between this life and the next should be folded like a flower in a night slumber, then the remembrance of the past might remain, as the smell and colour do in the sleeping flower; and in that case the memory of our love would last as true, and would live as pure and whole within the spirit of my friend until it was unfolded at the breaking of the morn, when the sleep was over." On the doctrine of soul sleep in the nineteenth century, see Shatto and Shaw 207, citing Isaac Taylor, *Physical Theory of Another Life* (1836), ch. 17: "We are also taught to think of the state of souls, as a state, not of unconsciousness indeed, but of comparative inaction, or of suspended energy.... The chrysalis period of the soul may be marked by the destitution of all the instruments of active life, corporeal and mental. And this state of inaction may probably also be a state of seclusion, involving, not improbably, an unconsciousness of the passage of time."

And silent traces of the past
Be all the colour of the flower:

So then were nothing lost to man;
    So that still garden of the souls   10
    In many a figured leaf enrolls
The total world since life began;

And love will last as pure and whole
    As when he loved me here in Time,
    And at the spiritual prime[1]   15
Rewaken with the dawning soul.

XLIV.

How fares it with the happy dead?
    For here the man is more and more;
    But he forgets the days before
God shut the doorways of his head.[2]

The days have vanish'd, tone and tint,   5
    And yet perhaps the hoarding sense
    Gives out at times (he knows not whence)
A little flash, a mystic hint;

And in the long harmonious years
    (If Death so taste Lethean springs),   10
    May some dim touch of earthly things
Surprise thee ranging with thy peers.

If such a dreamy touch should fall,
    O turn thee round, resolve the doubt;[3]

---

1 Morning.

2 "Closing of the skull after babyhood. The dead after this life may have
no remembrance of life, like the living babe who forgets the time before
the sutures of the skull are closed, yet the living babe grows in knowl-
edge, and though the remembrance of his earliest days has vanished, yet
with his increasing knowledge comes a dreamy vision of what has been;
it may be so with the dead; if so, resolve my doubts, etc." (T).

3 Tennyson said to James Knowles: "if you *have* forgot all earthly things—
yet as a man has faint memories, even so in the new life a sort of vague
memory of the past would come. This is fortified by considering that the
use of flesh & blood were lost if they do not establish an identity" (Ray
38). See also section 45.

My guardian angel will speak out   15
In that high place, and tell thee all.

XLV.

The baby new to earth and sky,
    What time his tender palm is prest
    Against the circle of the breast,
Has never thought that "this is I:"

But as he grows he gathers much,   5
    And learns the use of "I," and "me,"
    And finds "I am not what I see,
And other than the things I touch."

So rounds he to a separate mind
    From whence clear memory may begin,   10
    As thro' the frame that binds him in
His isolation grows defined.[1]

This use may lie in blood and breath,
    Which else were fruitless of their due,
    Had man to learn himself anew   15
Beyond the second birth of Death.

XLVI.

We ranging down this lower track,
    The path we came by, thorn and flower,
    Is shadow'd by the growing hour,
Lest life should fail in looking back.

So be it: there no shade can last   5
    In that deep dawn behind the tomb,
    But clear from marge to marge shall bloom
The eternal landscape of the past;

A lifelong tract of time reveal'd;[2]
    The fruitful hours of still increase;   10

---

1 Compare Arthur Hallam's account of how the infant develops con-
   sciousness of self and of others in his essay "On Sympathy," Appendix
   A4 (p. 149).

2 In life, as we move through time, we forget the past, and it falls into
   shadow behind us. To the dead, however, "the eternal land- (*continued*)

Days order'd in a wealthy peace,
And those five years its richest field.[1]

O Love, thy province were not large,
    A bounded field, nor stretching far;
    Look also, Love, a brooding star,   15
A rosy warmth from marge to marge.

XLVII.[2]

That each, who seems a separate whole,
    Should move his rounds, and fusing all
    The skirts of self again, should fall
Remerging in the general Soul,

Is faith as vague as all unsweet: 5
    Eternal form shall still divide
    The eternal soul from all beside;
And I shall know him when we meet:

And we shall sit at endless feast,
    Enjoying each the other's good: 10
    What vaster dream can hit the mood
Of Love on earth? He seeks at least

Upon the last and sharpest height,
    Before the spirits fade away,
    Some landing-place, to clasp and say,   15
"Farewell! We lose ourselves in light."

---

scape of the past" is visible as a single whole. The metaphor of the past
as a landscape is continued in the word "tract," which can mean a
stretch of land. It can also, however, refer to a book or pamphlet, so the
dead may read the past as well as view it.

1 Two manuscripts read "four years"; see also section 22.3 for Tennyson's
   lack of clarity about dates.

2 "The individuality lasts until after death, and we are not utterly
   absorbed into the Godhead. If we are to be finally merged in the Uni-
   versal Soul, Love asks to have at least one more parting before we lose
   ourselves" (T).

XLVIII.

If these brief lays, of Sorrow born,
    Were taken to be such as closed
    Grave doubts and answers here proposed,
Then these were such as men might scorn:

Her care is not to part and prove;   5
    She takes, when harsher moods remit,
    What slender shade of doubt may flit,
And makes it vassal unto love:

And hence, indeed, she sports with words,
    But better serves a wholesome law,   10
    And holds it sin and shame to draw
The deepest measure from the chords:

Nor dare she trust a larger lay,
    But rather loosens from the lip
    Short swallow-flights of song, that dip   15
Their wings in tears, and skim away.

XLIX.

From art, from nature, from the schools,
    Let random influences glance,
    Like light in many a shiver'd lance
That breaks about the dappled pools:

The lightest wave of thought shall lisp,   5
    The fancy's tenderest eddy wreathe,
    The slightest air of song shall breathe
To make the sullen surface crisp.

And look thy look, and go thy way,
    But blame not thou the winds that make   10
    The seeming-wanton ripple break,
The tender-pencil'd shadow play.

Beneath all fancied hopes and fears
    Ay me, the sorrow deepens down,
    Whose muffled motions blindly drown   15
The bases of my life in tears.

L.

Be near me when my light is low,
　　When the blood creeps, and the nerves prick
　　And tingle; and the heart is sick,
And all the wheels of Being slow.[1]

Be near me when the sensuous frame　　　　　　5
　　Is rack'd with pangs that conquer trust;
　　And Time, a maniac scattering dust,
And Life, a Fury slinging flame.

Be near me when my faith is dry,
　　And men the flies of latter spring,　　　　　　10
　　That lay their eggs, and sting and sing
And weave their petty cells and die.

Be near me when I fade away,
　　To point the term of human strife,
　　And on the low dark verge of life　　　　　　15
The twilight of eternal day.[2]

LI.

Do we indeed desire the dead
　　Should still be near us at our side?
　　Is there no baseness we would hide?
No inner vileness that we dread?

Shall he for whose applause I strove,　　　　　　5
　　I had such reverence for his blame,
　　See with clear eye some hidden shame
And I be lessen'd in his love?

I wrong the grave with fears untrue:
　　Shall love be blamed for want of faith?　　　　10
　　There must be wisdom with great Death:
The dead shall look me thro' and thro'.

1　Shelley, *Queen Mab* 9.151–52: "urge / the restless wheels of being on
　their way."

2　It is unclear how the word "twilight" fits into this section's syntax or
　what it represents. Is it the twilight of dawn or evening? How can there
　be twilight during an eternal day in any case?

Be near us when we climb or fall:
　　Ye watch, like God, the rolling hours
　　With larger other eyes than ours,   15
To make allowance for us all.

LII.

I cannot love thee as I ought,
　　For love reflects the thing beloved;
　　My words are only words, and moved
Upon the topmost froth of thought.

"Yet blame not thou thy plaintive song,"   5
　　The Spirit of true love replied;
　　"Thou canst not move me from thy side,
Nor human frailty do me wrong.

"What keeps a spirit wholly true
　　To that ideal which he bears?   10
　　What record? not the sinless years
That breathed beneath the Syrian blue:[1]

"So fret not, like an idle girl,
　　That life is dash'd with flecks of sin.
　　Abide: thy wealth is gather'd in,   15
When Time hath sunder'd shell from pearl."

LIII.

How many a father have I seen,
　　A sober man, among his boys,
　　Whose youth was full of foolish noise,
Who wears his manhood hale and green:

And dare we to this fancy give,   5
　　That had the wild oat not been sown,[2]

1　Nineteenth-century biblical criticism had shown that even the records of
　　Christ's life could not be "wholly true"; no more can the poet's words
　　be a full reflection of the man he loved.
2　To sow wild oats is a proverbial figure for youthful excess. See also
　　Matthew 13 for the parable of the seed and the sower.

The soil, left barren, scarce had grown
The grain by which a man may live?[1]

Or, if we held the doctrine sound
    For life outliving heats of youth,   10
    Yet who would preach it as a truth
To those that eddy round and round?

Hold thou the good: define it well:[2]
    For fear divine Philosophy[3]
    Should push beyond her mark, and be   15
Procuress to the Lords of Hell.

LIV.

Oh yet we trust that somehow good
    Will be the final goal of ill,
    To pangs of nature, sins of will,
Defects of doubt, and taints of blood;

That nothing walks with aimless feet;   5
    That not one life shall be destroy'd,
    Or cast as rubbish to the void,
When God hath made the pile complete;

That not a worm is cloven in vain;
    That not a moth with vain desire   10
    Is shrivell'd in a fruitless fire,[4]
Or but subserves another's gain.

---

1 "There is a passionate heat of nature in a rake sometimes. The nature
   that yields emotionally may turn out straighter than a prig's. Yet we must
   not be making excuses, but we must set before us a rule of good for
   young as for old" (T).
2 1 Thessalonians 5.21: "Prove all things; hold fast that which is good."
3 Milton, *Comus* 475: "How charming is divine philosophy!"
4 In his *Diary*, William Allingham recorded Tennyson asking: "'What do
   we know of the feelings of insects? Nothing. They may feel more pain
   than we.' On another occasion he commented on boys catching butter-
   flies: 'Why cut short their lives?—What are we? We are the merest moths
   ... Let the moths have their little lives'" (qtd. Shatto and Shaw 216).

Behold, we know not anything;
    I can but trust that good shall fall
    At last—far off—at last, to all,   15
And every winter change to spring.

So runs my dream: but what am I?
    An infant crying in the night:
    An infant crying for the light:
And with no language but a cry.[1]   20

LV.

The wish, that of the living whole
    No life may fail beyond the grave,
    Derives it not from what we have
The likest God within the soul?

Are God and Nature then at strife,   5
    That Nature lends such evil dreams?
    So careful of the type she seems,[2]
So careless of the single life;

That I, considering everywhere
    Her secret meaning in her deeds,   10
    And finding that of fifty seeds[3]
She often brings but one to bear,

I falter where I firmly trod,
    And falling with my weight of cares
    Upon the great world's altar-stairs   15
That slope thro' darkness up to God,

---

1 Jeremiah 1.6: "Then said I, Ah, Lord God! behold, I cannot speak: for I
   am a child." "Infans" in Latin means "unable to speak."
2 "Type" here refers to a species or class of living organisms. This sense of
   the word was introduced into English by natural historians during the
   1830s. In his *Philosophy of the Inductive Sciences* (1840) William Whewell,
   who had been Tennyson's tutor at Cambridge, proposed a system of
   classification in the life sciences based on *type species*. For other uses of
   the term "type" that may have influenced Tennyson, see the selections
   from Charles Lyell and Robert Chambers in Appendices B2 (p. 160)
   and B3 (p. 165).
3 "'Fifty' should be 'myriad'" (T).

I stretch lame hands of faith, and grope,
    And gather dust and chaff,[1] and call
    To what I feel is Lord of all,
And faintly trust the larger hope.   20

LVI.

"So careful of the type?" but no.
    From scarped cliff and quarried stone
    She cries,[2] "A thousand types are gone:
I care for nothing, all shall go.

"Thou makest thine appeal to me: 5
    I bring to life, I bring to death:
    The spirit does but mean the breath:[3]
I know no more." And he, shall he,

Man, her last work, who seem'd so fair,
    Such splendid purpose in his eyes,   10
    Who roll'd the psalm to wintry skies,
Who built him fanes of fruitless prayer,

Who trusted God was love indeed
    And love Creation's final law—
    Tho' Nature, red in tooth and claw   15
With ravine,[4] shriek'd against his creed—

Who loved, who suffer'd countless ills,
    Who battled for the True, the Just,

---

1 Chaff is the husk of a grain that is separated from the edible kernel by
   winnowing. The term can also refer to idle words or banter. It forms
   part of *In Memoriam*'s pattern of images using seed and sowing.

2 The comparative anatomist Georges Cuvier demonstrated in the 1790s
   that the fossil record contained the remains of species that had become
   extinct. The fact of extinction was broadly accepted among natural his-
   torians by the time of *In Memoriam*'s composition; for the geologist
   Charles Lyell's treatment of it, see Appendix B2 (p. 160).

3 The word "spirit" is etymologically a metaphor based on the Latin
   "spirare," to breathe.

4 This word, referring to the action of devouring prey, is usually spelled
   "ravin." "Ravine" is a term for "valley"; its odd appearance here sug-
   gests an echo of Shelley's word play on "rave" and "ravine" in "Mont
   Blanc," 11–48.

Be blown about the desert dust,
Or seal'd within the iron hills?   20

No more? A monster then, a dream,
        A discord. Dragons of the prime,[1]
        That tare each other in their slime,
Were mellow music match'd with him.

O life as futile, then, as frail!   25
        O for thy voice to soothe and bless!
        What hope of answer, or redress?
Behind the veil, behind the veil.[2]

LVII.[3]

Peace; come away: the song of woe
        Is after all an earthly song:
        Peace; come away: we do him wrong
To sing so wildly: let us go.

Come; let us go: your cheeks are pale;   5
        But half my life I leave behind:
        Methinks my friend is richly shrined;
But I shall pass; my work will fail.[4]

Yet in these ears, till hearing dies,
        One set slow bell will seem to toll   10
        The passing of the sweetest soul
That ever look'd with human eyes.

---

1   "The geologic monsters of the early ages" (T).

2   Plutarch writes in *Moralia* 354C that the Egyptian "temple of Minerva
    which is at Sais (whom they look upon as the same with Isis) had upon
    it this inscription, I am whatever was, or is, or will be; and my veil no
    mortal ever took up." Arthur Hallam alluded to this account in a sonnet
    to Emily Tennyson; see Appendix A2 (p. 149). There are many appear-
    ances of "veil" in Shelley; see especially "Mont Blanc" 53–54 where the
    verse paragraph on geology opens with the question: "Has some
    unknown omnipotence unfurled / The veil of life and death?"

3   Section 57 is the final poem of a fair copy of *In Memoriam* Tennyson
    made in the early 1840s. Shatto and Shaw conclude that he then
    intended it to close the sequence. Of the last stanza, he said to James
    Knowles "I thought this was too sad for an ending" (Ray 39).

4   "The poet speaks of these poems. Methinks I have built a rich shrine to
    my friend, but it will not last" (T).

I hear it now, and o'er and o'er,
    Eternal greetings to the dead;
    And "Ave, Ave, Ave," said,[1]   15
"Adieu, adieu" for evermore.[2]

LVIII.

In those sad words I took farewell:
    Like echoes in sepulchral halls,
    As drop by drop the water falls
In vaults and catacombs, they fell;

And, falling, idly broke the peace   5
    Of hearts that beat from day to day,
    Half-conscious of their dying clay,
And those cold crypts where they shall cease.

The high Muse answer'd: "Wherefore grieve
    Thy brethren with a fruitless tear?   10
    Abide a little longer here,
And thou shalt take a nobler leave."

LIX.[3]

O Sorrow, wilt thou live with me
    No casual mistress, but a wife,
    My bosom-friend and half of life;
As I confess it needs must be;

O Sorrow, wilt thou rule my blood,   5
    Be sometimes lovely like a bride,

---

1 Tennyson cites Catullus, poem 101, 9–10—referring to them as "these
    terribly pathetic lines 'Accipe fraterno multum manantia fletu, / atque in
    perpetuum, frater, ave atque vale' ['Take them, wet with many tears of a
    brother, and for ever, O my brother, hail and farewell!']." Hallam Ten-
    nyson adds, quoting a letter of his father to W.E. Gladstone: "My father
    wrote: 'Nor can any modern elegy, so long as men retain the least hope
    in the after-life of those whom they loved, equal in pathos the desolation
    of that everlasting farewell.'" Compare Tennyson's elegy on the death of
    his brother Charles in 1879, "Frater Ave Atque Vale."
2 Herbert Tucker notes the allusion to Keats's "Ode to a Nightingale" 75:
    "Adieu! Adieu!"
3 This section was added in the 4th edition (1851) as a pendant to
    section 3. Tennyson said to Knowles: "Added afterwards but one of the
    old poems nevertheless" (Ray 39).

And put thy harsher moods aside,
  If thou wilt have me wise and good.

My centred passion cannot move,
   Nor will it lessen from to-day;   10
   But I'll have leave at times to play
As with the creature of my love;

And set thee forth, for thou art mine,
   With so much hope for years to come,
   That, howsoe'er I know thee, some   15
Could hardly tell what name were thine.[1]

LX.

He past; a soul of nobler tone:
   My spirit loved and loves him yet,
   Like some poor girl whose heart is set
On one whose rank exceeds her own.

He mixing with his proper sphere,   5
   She finds the baseness of her lot,
   Half jealous of she knows not what,
And envying all that meet him there.

The little village looks forlorn;
   She sighs amid her narrow days,   10
   Moving about the household ways,
In that dark house where she was born.

The foolish neighbours come and go,
   And tease her till the day draws by:
   At night she weeps, "How vain am I! 15
How should he love a thing so low?"

LXI.

If, in thy second state sublime,
   Thy ransom'd reason change replies
   With all the circle of the wise,
The perfect flower of human time;

---

1 The speaker anticipates setting forth his sorrow in the sections that
 follow. In these, sorrow will appear with so much hope that some
 readers will hardly recognize her.

And if thou cast thine eyes below,   5
    How dimly character'd and slight,
    How dwarf'd a growth of cold and night,
How blanch'd with darkness must I grow!

Yet turn thee to the doubtful shore,
    Where thy first form was made a man;   10
    I loved thee, Spirit, and love, nor can
The soul of Shakspeare love thee more.

LXII.

Tho' if an eye that's downward cast
    Could make thee somewhat blench or fail,
    Then be my love an idle tale,
And fading legend of the past;

And thou, as one that once declined,   5
    When he was little more than boy,
    On some unworthy heart with joy,
But lives to wed an equal mind;

And breathes a novel world, the while
    His other passion wholly dies,   10
    Or in the light of deeper eyes
Is matter for a flying smile.

LXIII.

Yet pity for a horse o'er-driven,
    And love in which my hound has part,
    Can hang no weight upon my heart
In its assumptions up to heaven;

And I am so much more than these,   5
    As thou, perchance, art more than I,
    And yet I spare them sympathy,
And I would set their pains at ease.

So mayst thou watch me where I weep,
    As, unto vaster motions bound,   10
    The circuits of thine orbit round
A higher height, a deeper deep.

LXIV.[1]

Dost thou look back on what hath been,
    As some divinely gifted man,
    Whose life in low estate began[2]
And on a simple village green;

Who breaks his birth's invidious bar,   5
    And grasps the skirts of happy chance,
    And breasts the blows of circumstance,
And grapples with his evil star;

Who makes by force his merit known
    And lives to clutch the golden keys,   10
    To mould a mighty state's decrees,
And shape the whisper of the throne;

And moving up from high to higher,
    Becomes on Fortune's crowning slope
    The pillar of a people's hope,   15
The centre of a world's desire;

Yet feels, as in a pensive dream,
    When all his active powers are still,
    A distant dearness in the hill,
A secret sweetness in the stream,   20

The limit of his narrower fate,
    While yet beside its vocal springs
    He play'd at counsellors and kings,[3]
With one that was his earliest mate;

Who ploughs with pain his native lea   25
    And reaps the labour of his hands,
    Or in the furrow musing stands;
"Does my old friend remember me?"

---

1 The metaphor we are given for Hallam's life after death in this section
    ironically suggests what he might have achieved had he lived. Compare
    section 113.
2 Psalm 136.23: "Who remembered us in our low estate."
3 Job 3.14: "kings and counsellors of the earth."

LXV.

Sweet soul, do with me as thou wilt;
    I lull a fancy trouble-tost
    With "Love's too precious to be lost,
A little grain shall not be spilt."[1]

And in that solace can I sing,   5
    Till out of painful phases wrought
    There flutters up a happy thought,
Self-balanced on a lightsome wing:

Since we deserved the name of friends,
    And thine effect so lives in me,   10
    A part of mine may live in thee
And move thee on to noble ends.

LXVI.

You thought my heart too far diseased;
    You wonder when my fancies play
    To find me gay among the gay,
Like one with any trifle pleased.

The shade by which my life was crost,   5
    Which makes a desert in the mind,
    Has made me kindly with my kind,
And like to him whose sight is lost;

Whose feet are guided thro' the land,
    Whose jest among his friends is free,   10
    Who takes the children on his knee,
And winds their curls about his hand:

He plays with threads, he beats his chair
    For pastime, dreaming of the sky;
    His inner day can never die,   15
His night of loss is always there.

---

1 For the image of love as grain, see also section 81.

LXVII.

When on my bed the moonlight falls,
    I know that in thy place of rest
    By that broad water of the west,[1]
There comes a glory on the walls;

Thy marble bright in dark appears,[2]   5
    As slowly steals a silver flame
    Along the letters of thy name,
And o'er the number of thy years.

The mystic glory swims away;
    From off my bed the moonlight dies;   10
    And closing eaves of wearied eyes
I sleep till dusk is dipt in gray:

And then I know the mist is drawn
    A lucid veil from coast to coast,[3]
    And in the dark church like a ghost   15
Thy tablet glimmers to the dawn.[4]

LXVIII.

When in the down I sink my head,
    Sleep, Death's twin-brother, times my breath;[5]
    Sleep, Death's twin-brother, knows not Death,
Nor can I dream of thee as dead:

---

1 "The Severn" (T).

2 Shakespeare, *Sonnets* 43.4: "And darkly bright, are bright in dark directed."

3 See Ricks for sources and analogues of the phrase "lucid veil." The word "lucid" derives from the Latin "lucere," meaning "to shine." Its primary sense in English is "transparent" or "clear"; it is often used in a figural sense to describe speech or writing.

4 "I myself did not see Clevedon till years after the burial of A.H.H. (Jan. 3, 1834), and then in later editions of *In Memoriam* I altered the word 'chancel' ... to 'dark church'" (T). Tennyson visited the church at Clevedon on his honeymoon in June 1850 and learned that Hallam's tomb was not in the chancel but in the transept. He changed line 15 to read "dark church" for the 6th edition in 1855.

5 Tennyson refers to Virgil, *Aeneid* 6.278: "Consanguineus Leti Sopor [Death's own brother Sleep]."

I walk as ere I walk'd forlorn,   5
    When all our path was fresh with dew,
    And all the bugle breezes blew
Reveillée to the breaking morn.

But what.is this? I turn about,
    I find a trouble in thine eye,   10
    Which makes me sad I know not why,
Nor can my dream resolve the doubt:

But ere the lark hath left the lea
    I wake, and I discern the truth;
    It is the trouble of my youth   15
That foolish sleep transfers to thee.

LXIX.[1]

I dream'd there would be Spring no more,
    That Nature's ancient power was lost:
    The streets were black with smoke and frost,
They chatter'd trifles at the door:

I wander'd from the noisy town,   5
    I found a wood with thorny boughs:
    I took the thorns to bind my brows,
I wore them like a civic crown:

I met with scoffs, I met with scorns
    From youth and babe and hoary hairs: 10
    They call'd me in the public squares
The fool that wears a crown of thorns:[2]

They call'd me fool, they call'd me child:
    I found an angel of the night;[3]
    The voice was low, the look was bright;   15
He look'd upon my crown and smiled:

He reach'd the glory of a hand,
    That seem'd to touch it into leaf:

---

1 "To write a poem about death and grief is 'to wear a crown of thorns,' which the people say ought to be laid aside" (T).

2 For Jesus' crown of thorns, see Matthew 27, Mark 15, and John 19.

3 "But the Divine Thing in the gloom brought comfort" (T).

The voice was not the voice of grief,
    The words were hard to understand.   20

LXX.

I cannot see the features right,
    When on the gloom I strive to paint
    The face I know; the hues are faint
And mix with hollow masks of night;

Cloud-towers by ghostly masons wrought,   5
    A gulf that ever shuts and gapes,
    A hand that points, and palled shapes
In shadowy thoroughfares of thought;

And crowds that stream from yawning doors,
    And shoals of pucker'd faces drive;   10
    Dark bulks that tumble half alive,
And lazy lengths on boundless shores;[1]

Till all at once beyond the will
    I hear a wizard music roll,
    And thro' a lattice on the soul   15
Looks thy fair face and makes it still.

LXXI.

Sleep, kinsman thou to death and trance
    And madness, thou hast forged at last
    A night-long Present of the Past
In which we went thro' summer France.[2]

Hadst thou such credit with the soul?[3]   5
    Then bring an opiate trebly strong,

---

1 See Shatto and Shaw 230 for comparison of stanzas 2 and 3 with the
descent to Hades in Virgil, *Aeneid* 6, and Christopher Ricks for echoes
of Thomas Carlyle's *The French Revolution* (1837).

2 In the summer of 1830 Tennyson and Hallam traveled to the south of
France to meet with insurgents against the Spanish monarchy. They
carried funds raised by British liberals and dispatches from the insur-
gency's exiled leader, General José Torrijos. For another poem recalling
this summer, see "In the Valley of Cauteretz" (1864).

3 The speaker asks Sleep, "Did you really persuade my soul that the past
was present again?" Now he feels a "sense of wrong" in the memory of
his dream.

Drug down the blindfold sense of wrong
That so my pleasure may be whole;

While now we talk as once we talk'd
  Of men and minds, the dust of change,
  The days that grow to something strange,
In walking as of old we walk'd

Beside the river's wooded reach,
  The fortress, and the mountain ridge,
  The cataract flashing from the bridge,
The breaker breaking on the beach.

LXXII.[1]

Risest thou thus, dim dawn, again,
  And howlest, issuing out of night,
  With blasts that blow the poplar white,
And lash with storm the streaming pane?

Day, when my crown'd estate begun
  To pine in that reverse of doom,
  Which sicken'd every living bloom,
And blurr'd the splendour of the sun;

Who usherest in the dolorous hour
  With thy quick tears that make the rose
  Pull sideways, and the daisy close
Her crimson fringes to the shower;

Who might'st have heaved a windless flame
  Up the deep East, or, whispering, play'd
  A chequer-work of beam and shade
Along the hills, yet look'd the same,

As wan, as chill, as wild as now;
  Day, mark'd as with some hideous crime,
  When the dark hand struck down thro' time,
And cancell'd nature's best:[2] but thou,

---

1   "Hallam's death-day, September the 15th" (T).
2   "To cancel" means to cross out or mark for deletion.

Lift as thou may'st thy burthen'd brows
    Thro' clouds that drench the morning star,
    And whirl the ungarner'd sheaf afar,
And sow the sky with flying boughs,

And up thy vault with roaring sound   25
    Climb thy thick noon, disastrous day;[1]
    Touch thy dull goal of joyless gray,
And hide thy shame beneath the ground.

LXXIII.

So many worlds, so much to do,
    So little done, such things to be,
    How know I what had need of thee,
For thou wert strong as thou wert true?

The fame is quench'd that I foresaw,   5
    The head hath miss'd an earthly wreath:
    I curse not nature, no, nor death;
For nothing is that errs from law.

We pass; the path that each man trod
    Is dim, or will be dim, with weeds: 10
    What fame is left for human deeds
In endless age? It rests with God.

O hollow wraith of dying fame,
    Fade wholly, while the soul exults,
    And self-infolds the large results   15
Of force that would have forged a name.

LXXIV.

As sometimes in a dead man's face,
    To those that watch it more and more,
    A likeness, hardly seen before,
Comes out—to some one of his race:[2]

---

1 "Disastrous," from the Latin "astrum," or star: literally, a day without a
    star.
2 See Shatto and Shaw 232; they cite Sir Thomas Browne, who wrote in
    "Letter to a Friend" of someone near death: "He lost his own face, and
    looked like one of his near relations."

So, dearest,[1] now thy brows are cold,
    I see thee what thou art, and know
    Thy likeness to the wise below,
Thy kindred with the great of old.   5

But there is more than I can see,
    And what I see I leave unsaid,
    Nor speak it, knowing Death has made   10
His darkness beautiful with thee.[2]

LXXV.

I leave thy praises unexpress'd
    In verse that brings myself relief,
    And by the measure of my grief
I leave thy greatness to be guess'd;

What practice howsoe'er expert   5
    In fitting aptest words to things,
    Or voice the richest-toned that sings,
Hath power to give thee as thou wert?

I care not in these fading days
    To raise a cry that lasts not long,   10
    And round thee with the breeze of song
To stir a little dust of praise.

Thy leaf has perish'd in the green,
    And, while we breathe beneath the sun,
    The world which credits what is done   15
Is cold to all that might have been.

So here shall silence guard thy fame;
    But somewhere, out of human view,
    Whate'er thy hands are set to do
Is wrought with tumult of acclaim.   20

---

1   Tennyson said to James Knowles: "If anybody thinks I ever called him
    'dearest' in his life they are much mistaken, for I never even called him
    'dear'" (Knowles 187).
2   Petrarch, *Sonnets to Laura in Death* (*Canzoniere* 358) "Non pò far Morte
    il dolce viso amaro, / ma 'l dolce viso dolce pò far Morte." In his essay
    on "The Influence of Italian upon English Literature" Hallam translated

LXXVI.

Take wings of fancy, and ascend,
  And in a moment set thy face
  Where all the starry heavens of space
Are sharpen'd to a needle's end;

Take wings of foresight; lighten thro'   5
  The secular abyss to come,[1]
  And lo, thy deepest lays are dumb
Before the mouldering of a yew;

And if the matin songs,[2] that woke
  The darkness of our planet, last,   10
  Thine own shall wither in the vast,
Ere half the lifetime of an oak.

Ere these have clothed their branchy bowers
  With fifty Mays, thy songs are vain;
  And what are they when these remain   15
The ruin'd shells of hollow towers?

LXXVII.

What hope is here for modern rhyme
  To him, who turns a musing eye
  On songs, and deeds, and lives, that lie
Foreshorten'd in the tract of time?

These mortal lullabies of pain   5
  May bind a book, may line a box,
  May serve to curl a maiden's locks;[3]
Or when a thousand moons shall wane

A man upon a stall may find,
  And, passing, turn the page that tells   10
  A grief, then changed to something else,
Sung by a long-forgotten mind.

---

the second line as "Death appeared lovely in that lovely face" (T.H. Vail
Motter, ed., *The Writings of Arthur Hallam* [New York: Modern Language
Association, 1943], 225).

1 "The ages upon ages to be" (T).
2 "The great early poets" (T).
3 Waste paper from remaindered or discarded books might have been
  used in new book bindings, in trunk liners, or to curl hair.

But what of that? My darken'd ways
    Shall ring with music all the same;
    To breathe my loss is more than fame,   15
To utter love more sweet than praise.[1]

LXXVIII.[2]

Again at Christmas did we weave
    The holly round the Christmas hearth;
    The silent snow possess'd the earth,
And calmly fell our Christmas eve:

The yule-clog[3] sparkled keen with frost,   5
    No wing of wind the region swept,
    But over all things brooding slept
The quiet sense of something lost.

As in the winters left behind,
    Again our ancient games had place,   10
    The mimic picture's breathing grace,
And dance and song and hoodman-blind.[4]

Who show'd a token of distress?
    No single tear, no mark of pain:
    O sorrow, then can sorrow wane?   15
O grief, can grief be changed to less?

O last regret, regret can die!
    No—mixt with all this mystic frame,
    Her deep relations are the same,
But with long use her tears are dry.   20

---

1 Petrarch, *Sonnets to Laura in Death* 'Si io avesse pensato che sì care' (*Canzoniere* 293) 9–12: "ogni mio studio in quel tempo era / pur di sfogare il doloroso core / in qualche modo, non d'aquisitar fama. / Pianger cercai, non già del pianto onore [all my effort in that time was only to express my grieving heart in some way, not to get fame. I sought to weep, not to get honor by weeping]."

2 In the internal chronology of the poem, the second Christmas Eve after Hallam's death. Compare to sections 30 and 105.

3 In Lincolnshire and northern England, "clog" is a dialect word for "log."

4 Tableaux vivants and blindman's buff are party games.

LXXIX.[1]

"More than my brothers are to me,"—[2]
    Let this not vex thee, noble heart!
    I know thee of what force thou art
To hold the costliest love in fee.

But thou and I are one in kind,   5
    As moulded like in Nature's mind;
    And hill and wood and field did print
The same sweet forms in either mind.

For us the same cold streamlet curl'd
    Thro' all his eddying coves; the same   10
    All winds that roam the twilight came
In whispers of the beauteous world.

At one dear knee we proffer'd vows,
    One lesson from one book we learn'd,
    Ere childhood's flaxen ringlet turn'd   15
To black and brown on kindred brows.

And so my wealth resembles thine,
    But he was rich where I was poor,
    And he supplied my want the more
As his unlikeness fitted mine.   20

LXXX.

If any vague desire should rise,
    That holy Death ere Arthur died
    Had moved me kindly from his side,
And dropt the dust on tearless eyes;

Then fancy shapes, as fancy can,   5
    The grief my loss in him had wrought,
    A grief as deep as life or thought,
But stay'd in peace with god and man.

I make a picture in the brain;
    I hear the sentence that he speaks;   10

---

1 "This section is addressed to my brother Charles (Tennyson Turner)"
(T).

2 Here Tennyson quotes himself from section 9.20.

He bears the burthen of the weeks
But turns his burthen into gain.

His credit thus shall set me free;
    And, influence-rich to soothe and save,
    Unused example from the grave   15
Reach out dead hands to comfort me.[1]

LXXXI.

Could I have said while he was here,[2]
    "My love shall now no further range;
    There cannot come a mellower change,
For now is love mature in ear."

Love, then, had hope of richer store: 5
    What end is here to my complaint?
    This haunting whisper makes me faint,
"More years had made me love thee more."

But Death returns an answer sweet:
    "My sudden frost was sudden gain,   10
    And gave all ripeness to the grain,
It might have drawn from after-heat."

LXXXII.

I wage not any feud with Death
    For changes wrought on form and face;
    No lower life that earth's embrace
May breed with him, can fright my faith.

Eternal process moving on,   5
    From state to state the spirit walks;
    And these are but the shatter'd stalks,
Or ruin'd chrysalis of one.

Nor blame I Death, because he bare
    The use of virtue out of earth: 10

---

1 The economic metaphor and the image of hands reaching through time
   link this to section 1.
2 "=Would that I could have said, etc." (T). For extended comment on
   the difficult syntactical and logical relation between stanzas 1 and 2 see
   Bradley, and Shatto and Shaw.

I know transplanted human worth
Will bloom to profit, otherwhere.

For this alone on Death I wreak
　　The wrath that garners in my heart;
　　He put our lives so far apart　　　　　　　　　15
We cannot hear each other speak.

LXXXIII.

Dip down upon the northern shore,
　　O sweet new-year[1] delaying long;
　　Thou doest expectant nature wrong;
Delaying long, delay no more.[2]

What stays thee from the clouded noons,　　　　5
　　Thy sweetness from its proper place?
　　Can trouble live with April days,
Or sadness in the summer moons?

Bring orchis, bring the foxglove spire,
　　The little speedwell's darling blue,　　　　　10
　　Deep tulips dash'd with fiery dew,
Laburnums, dropping-wells of fire.[3]

O thou, new-year, delaying long,
　　Delayest the sorrow in my blood,
　　That longs to burst a frozen bud[4]　　　　　15
And flood a fresher throat with song.

LXXXIV.

When I contemplate all alone
　　The life that had been thine below,
　　And fix my thoughts on all the glow
To which thy crescent would have grown;[5]

1　Until 1751 the English new year began on 25 March; in this section
　　Tennyson retains the old usage and identifies the coming of the new
　　year with the coming of spring.

2　Shelley, *Prometheus Unbound* 2.1.15: "Too long desired, too long delay-
　　ing, come!"

3　Compare the flower catalogue in Milton, "Lycidas" 142–51.

4　Shelley, "Epipsychidion" 110–11: "like fiery dews that melt / Into the
　　bosom of a frozen bud."

5　Shelley, "Adonais" 241–42: "Or hadst thou waited the full cycle, when /
　　Thy spirit should have filled its crescent sphere."

I see thee sitting crown'd with good,   5
     A central warmth diffusing bliss
     In glance and smile, and clasp and kiss,
On all the branches of thy blood;

Thy blood, my friend, and partly mine;
     For now the day was drawing on,   10
     When thou should'st link thy life with one
Of mine own house,[1] and boys of thine

Had babbled "Uncle" on my knee;
     But that remorseless iron hour
     Made cypress of her orange flower,   15
Despair of Hope, and earth of thee.

I seem to meet their least desire,
     To clap their cheeks, to call them mine.
     I see their unborn faces shine
Beside the never-lighted fire.   20

I see myself an honour'd guest,
     Thy partner in the flowery walk
     Of letters, genial table-talk,
Or deep dispute, and graceful jest:

While now thy prosperous labour fills   25
     The lips of men with honest praise,
     And sun by sun the happy days
Descend below the golden hills

With promise of a morn as fair;
     And all the train of bounteous hours   30
     Conduct by paths of growing powers,
To reverence and the silver hair;

Till slowly worn her earthly robe,
     Her lavish mission richly wrought,
     Leaving great legacies of thought,   35
Thy spirit should fail from off the globe;

---

1 "The projected marriage of A.H.H. with Emily Tennyson" (T).

What time mine own might also flee,
    As link'd with thine in love and fate,
    And, hovering o'er the dolorous strait
To the other shore, involved in thee,   40

Arrive at last the blessed goal,[1]
    And He that died in Holy Land
    Would reach us out the shining hand,
And take us as a single soul.

What reed was that on which I leant?   45
    Ah, backward fancy, wherefore wake
    The old bitterness again, and break
The low beginnings of content.

LXXXV.[2]

This truth came borne with bier and pall,
    I felt it, when I sorrow'd most,
    'Tis better to have loved and lost,
Than never to have loved at all——[3]

O true in word, and tried in deed,   5
    Demanding, so to bring relief
    To this which is our common grief,
What kind of life is that I lead;

And whether trust in things above
    Be dimm'd of sorrow, or sustain'd;   10
    And whether love for him have drain'd
My capabilities of love;

---

1 To illustrate this use of "arrive," Tennyson cites Milton, *Paradise Lost* 2.409–10: "ere he arrive / The happy isle."

2 Hallam Tennyson writes that this section is "addressed to Edmund Lushington," whom Tennyson knew from Cambridge and whose wedding to Cecilia Tennyson is celebrated in the epithalamium at *In Memoriam*'s close. The manuscript evidence, however, shows that the poem was written at different periods, and may have been addressed to different men, or, in the earliest written parts, to an imaginary friend. See Shatto and Shaw 239 for confusion among the early commentators about whether this section, especially the lines beginning 113, refers to a man or a woman.

3 Quoted from section 27.

Your words have virtue such as draws
    A faithful answer from the breast,
    Thro' light reproaches, half exprest,   15
And loyal unto kindly laws.

My blood an even tenor kept,
    Till on mine ear this message falls,
    That in Vienna's fatal walls
God's finger touch'd him, and he slept.   20

The great Intelligences fair
    That range above our mortal state,[1]
    In circle round the blessed gate,
Received and gave him welcome there;[2]

And led him thro' the blissful climes,   25
    And show'd him in the fountain fresh
    All knowledge that the sons of flesh
Shall gather in the cycled times.

But I remain'd, whose hopes were dim,
    Whose life, whose thoughts were little worth,   30
    To wander on a darken'd earth,
Where all things round me breathed of him.

O friendship, equal-poised control,
    O heart, with kindliest motion warm,
    O sacred essence, other form,   35
O solemn ghost, O crowned soul!

Yet none could better know than I,
    How much of act at human hands
    The sense of human will demands
By which we dare to live or die.[3]   40

---

1 Dante, *Convito* 2.5: "Intelligenze, le quali la volgare gente chiama Angeli [Intelligences, whom the vulgar call angels]."

2 Tennyson compares Milton, "Lycidas" 178–81: "There entertain him all the saints above, / In solemn troops, and sweet societies / That sing, and singing in their glory move, / And wipe the tears forever from his eyes."

3 "Yet I know that the knowledge we have free will demands from us action" (T).

Whatever way my days decline,
  I felt and feel, tho' left alone,
  His being working in mine own,
The footsteps of his life in mine;

A life that all the Muses deck'd   45
  With gifts of grace, that might express
  All-comprehensive tenderness,
All-subtilising intellect:

And so my passion hath not swerved
  To works of weakness, but I find   50
  An image comforting the mind,
And in my grief a strength reserved.

Likewise the imaginative woe,
  That loved to handle spiritual strife
  Diffused the shock thro' all my life, 55
But in the present broke the blow.

My pulses therefore beat again
  For other friends that once I met;
  Nor can it suit me to forget
The mighty hopes that make us men. 60

I woo your love: I count it crime
  To mourn for any overmuch;
  I, the divided half of such
A friendship as had master'd Time;

Which masters Time indeed, and is 65
  Eternal, separate from fears:
  The all-assuming months and years
Can take no part away from this:

But Summer on the steaming floods,
  And Spring that swells the narrow brooks, 70
  And Autumn, with a noise of rooks,
That gather in the waning woods,

And every pulse of wind and wave
  Recalls, in change of light or gloom,
  My old affection of the tomb, 75
And my prime passion in the grave:

My old affection of the tomb,
    A part of stillness, yearns to speak:
    "Arise, and get thee forth and seek
A friendship for the years to come.   80

"I watch thee from the quiet shore;
  ·   Thy spirit up to mine can reach;
    But in dear words of human speech
We two communicate no more."

And I, "Can clouds of nature stain   85
    The starry clearness of the free?
    How is it? Canst thou feel for me
Some painless sympathy with pain?"

And lightly does the whisper fall;
    "'Tis hard for thee to fathom this;   90
    I triumph in conclusive bliss,
And that serene result of all."

So hold I commerce with the dead;
    Or so methinks the dead would say;
    Or so shall grief with symbols play   95
And pining life be fancy-fed.

Now looking to some settled end,
    That these things pass, and I shall prove
    A meeting somewhere, love with love,
I crave your pardon, O my friend;   100

If not so fresh, with love as true,
    I, clasping brother-hands, aver
    I could not, if I would, transfer
The whole I felt for him to you.

For which be they that hold apart   105
    The promise of the golden hours?
    First love, first friendship, equal powers,
That marry with the virgin heart.

Still mine, that cannot but deplore,
    That beats within a lonely place,   110
    That yet remembers his embrace,
But at his footstep leaps no more,

My heart, tho' widow'd, may not rest
    Quite in the love of what is gone,
    But seeks to beat in time with one   115
That warms another living breast.

Ah, take the imperfect gift I bring,
    Knowing the primrose yet is dear,
    The primrose of the later year,
As not unlike to that of Spring.

LXXXVI.[1]

Sweet after showers, ambrosial air,
    That rollest from the gorgeous gloom
    Of evening over brake and bloom
And meadow, slowly breathing bare

The round of space, and rapt below   5
    Thro' all the dewy-tassell'd wood,
    And shadowing down the horned flood[2]
In ripples, fan my brows and blow

The fever from my cheek, and sigh
    The full new life that feeds thy breath   10
    Throughout my frame, till Doubt and Death,
Ill brethren, let the fancy fly

From belt to belt of crimson seas
    On leagues of odour streaming far,
    To where in yonder orient star   15
A hundred spirits whisper "Peace."

LXXXVII.[3]

I past beside the reverend walls
    In which of old I wore the gown;
    I roved at random thro' the town,
And saw the tumult of the halls;

---

1 "Written at Barmouth" (T). Bradley notes that Barmouth is famed for
    its sunsets over the estuary.
2 "Between two promontories" (T). Shatto and Shaw note that the phrase
    is a Latin commonplace; it also appears in Ben Jonson, Thomas Browne,
    and Milton. "Horned" is pronounced with two syllables.
3 "Trinity College, Cambridge" (T).

And heard once more in college fanes[1]   5
    The storm their high-built organs make,
    And thunder-music, rolling, shake
The prophet blazon'd on the panes;

And caught once more the distant shout,
    The measured pulse of racing oars   10
    Among the willows; paced the shores
And many a bridge, and all about

The same gray flats again, and felt
    The same, but not the same; and last
    Up that long walk of limes I past   15
To see the rooms in which he dwelt.

Another name was on the door:
    I linger'd; all within was noise
    Of songs, and clapping hands, and boys
That crash'd the glass and beat the floor;   20

Where once we held debate, a band
    Of youthful friends, on mind and art,
    And labour, and the changing mart,
And all the framework of the land;

When one would aim an arrow fair,   25
    But send it slackly from the string;
    And one would pierce an outer ring,
And one an inner, here and there;

And last the master-bowman, he,
    Would cleave the mark. A willing ear   30
    We lent him. Who, but hung to hear
The rapt oration flowing free

From point to point, with power and grace
    And music in the bounds of law,
    To those conclusions when we saw   35
The God within him light his face,

---

1 Literally, temples: here, college chapels.

And seem to lift the form, and glow
    In azure orbits heavenly-wise;
    And over those ethereal eyes
The bar of Michael Angelo.[1]   40

LXXXVIII.[2]

Wild bird, whose warble, liquid sweet,
    Rings Eden thro' the budded quicks,[3]
    O tell me where the senses mix,
O tell me where the passions meet,

Whence radiate: fierce extremes employ   5
    Thy spirits in the darkening leaf,
    And in the midmost heart of grief
Thy passion clasps a secret joy:

And I—my harp would prelude woe—[4]
    I cannot all command the strings;   10
    The glory of the sum of things
Will flash along the chords and go.

LXXXIX.[5]

Witch-elms that counterchange[6] the floor
    Of this flat lawn with dusk and bright;
    And thou, with all thy breadth and height
Of foliage, towering sycamore;

---

1 "The broad bar of frontal bone over the eyes of Michael Angelo" (T). In
    the *Memoir* Tennyson recalls: "These lines I wrote from what Arthur
    Hallam said after reading of the prominent ridge of bone over the eyes
    of Michael Angelo: 'Alfred, look over my eyes; surely I have the bar of
    Michael Angelo!'" (1.38).
2 "To the Nightingale" (T).
3 Hawthorn or other flowering hedge made with quick-sets (cuttings).
4 When he draws an analogy between his poetry and the nightingale's
    song, Tennyson gives a new twist to a traditional image. For famous
    earlier examples, see Keats's "Ode to a Nightingale," Shelley's "Defence
    of Poetry," and the invocation to Book 3 of Milton's *Paradise Lost*. To
    understand the nightingale's grief, consult the story of Philomela; the
    most influential telling is in Ovid, *Metamorphoses* 6.438–674.
5 "Somersby" (T). The rectory there was Tennyson's birthplace and his
    family's home until 1837. This section commemorates Hallam's visits
    during the summers of 1832 and 1833, while he was living in London
    and preparing for a legal career.
6 A heraldic term meaning to chequer.

How often, hither wandering down,   5
    My Arthur found your shadows fair,
    And shook to all the liberal air
The dust and din and steam of town:

He brought an eye for all he saw;
    He mixt in all our simple sports;   10
    They pleased him, fresh from brawling courts
And dusty purlieus of the law.

O joy to him in this retreat,
    Immantled in ambrosial dark,
    To drink the cooler air, and mark   15
The landscape winking thro' the heat:

O sound to rout the brood of cares,
    The sweep of scythe in morning dew,
    The gust that round the garden flew,
And tumbled half the mellowing pears!   20

O bliss, when all in circle drawn
    About him, heart and ear were fed
    To hear him, as he lay and read
The Tuscan poets on the lawn:

Or in the all-golden afternoon   25
    A guest, or happy sister, sung,
    Or here she brought the harp and flung
A ballad to the brightening moon:

Nor less it pleased in livelier moods,
    Beyond the bounding hill to stray,   30
    And break the livelong summer day
With banquet in the distant woods;

Whereat we glanced from theme to theme,
    Discuss'd the books to love or hate,
    Or touch'd the changes of the state,   35
Or threaded some Socratic dream;

But if I praised the busy town,
    He loved to rail against it still,
    For "ground in yonder social mill
We rub each other's angles down,   40

"And merge" he said "in form and gloss
        The picturesque of man and man."
        We talk'd: the stream beneath us ran,
The wine-flask lying couch'd in moss,

Or cool'd within the glooming wave;   45
        And last, returning from afar,
        Before the crimson-circled star
Had fall'n into her father's grave,[1]

And brushing ankle-deep in flowers,
        We heard behind the woodbine veil   50
        The milk that bubbled in the pail,
And buzzings of the honied hours.

XC.

He tasted love with half his mind,
        Nor ever drank the inviolate spring
        Where nighest heaven, who first could fling
This bitter seed among mankind;

That could the dead, whose dying eyes   5
        Were closed with wail, resume their life,
        They would but find in child and wife
An iron welcome when they rise:[2]

'Twas well, indeed, when warm with wine,
        To pledge them with a kindly tear,   10
        To talk them o'er, to wish them here,
To count their memories half divine;

But if they came who past away,
        Behold their brides in other hands;

---

1   "Before Venus, the evening star, had dipped into the sunset. The planets,
    according to Laplace, were evolved from the sun" (T). Pierre-Simon
    Laplace (1749–1827) was the most important cosmologist of his time
    and a proponent of the nebular hypothesis of planetary development.
2   The cold welcome the dead might receive if they returned is a recurrent
    theme in Tennyson. See "The Lotos-Eaters" 117–19: "For surely now
    our household hearths are cold: / Our sons inherit us: our looks are
    strange: / And we should come like ghosts to trouble joy." "Enoch
    Arden" also treats this theme.

The hard heir strides about their lands,   15
And will not yield them for a day.

Yea, tho' their sons were none of these,
        Not less the yet-loved sire would make
        Confusion worse than death, and shake
The pillars of domestic peace.   20

Ah dear, but come thou back to me:
        Whatever change the years have wrought,
        I find not yet one lonely thought
That cries against my wish for thee.

XCI.[1]

When rosy plumelets tuft the larch,
        And rarely pipes the mounted thrush;
        Or underneath the barren bush
Flits by the sea-blue bird of March;[2]

Come, wear the form by which I know   5
        Thy spirit in time among thy peers;
        The hope of unaccomplish'd years
Be large and lucid round thy brow.

When summer's hourly-mellowing change
        May breathe, with many roses sweet,   10
        Upon the thousand waves of wheat,
That ripple round the lonely grange;

Come: not in watches of the night,
        But where the sunbeam broodeth warm,
        Come, beauteous in thine after form,   15
And like a finer light in light.

XCII.

If any vision should reveal
        Thy likeness, I might count it vain
        As but the canker of the brain;
Yea, tho' it spake and made appeal

---

1 This section echoes the form of Shakespeare's song "When daisies pied"
   at the end of *Love's Labour's Lost* (5.2.894–929).
2 The kingfisher.

To chances where our lots were cast 5
Together in the days behind,
I might but say, I hear a wind
Of memory murmuring the past.

Yea, tho' it spake and bared to view
A fact within the coming year; 10
And tho' the months, revolving near,
Should prove the phantom-warning true,

They might not seem thy prophecies,
But spiritual presentiments,
And such refraction of events 15
As often rises ere they rise.[1]

XCIII.

I shall not see thee. Dare I say
No spirit ever brake the band
That stays him from the native land
Where first he walk'd when claspt in clay?

No visual shade of some one lost, 5
But he, the Spirit himself, may come
Where all the nerve of sense is numb;
Spirit to Spirit, Ghost to Ghost.

O, therefore from thy sightless[2] range
With gods in unconjectured bliss, 10
O, from the distance of the abyss
Of tenfold-complicated change,

Descend, and touch, and enter; hear[3]
The wish too strong for words to name;
That in this blindness of the frame 15
My Ghost may feel that thine is near.

---

1 "The heavenly bodies are seen above the horizon, by refraction, before
they actually rise" (T).
2 Invisible.
3 The two manuscripts for this section record Tennyson's first version of
these lines: "Stoop soul & touch me: wed me: hear / The wish too strong
for words to name."

XCIV.

How pure at heart and sound in head,
    With what divine affections bold
    Should be the man whose thought would hold
An hour's communion with the dead.

In vain shalt thou, or any, call   5
    The spirits from their golden day,
    Except, like them, thou too canst say,
My spirit is at peace with all.

They haunt the silence of the breast,
    Imaginations calm and fair,   10
    The memory like a cloudless air,
The conscience as a sea at rest:

But when the heart is full of din,
    And doubt beside the portal waits,
    They can but listen at the gates,   15
And hear the household jar within.

XCV.

By night we linger'd on the lawn,
    For underfoot the herb was dry;
    And genial warmth; and o'er the sky
The silvery haze of summer drawn;

And calm that let the tapers burn   5
    Unwavering: not a cricket chirr'd:
    The brook alone far-off was heard,
And on the board the fluttering urn:

And bats went round in fragrant skies,
    And wheel'd or lit[1] the filmy shapes   10
    That haunt the dusk, with ermine capes
And woolly breasts and beaded eyes;[2]

---

1 Alighted.

2 "Moths; perhaps the ermine or the puss-moth" (T). In section 54, the
    moth that flies into a flame is a figure of fruitless desire. Here the moths
    remain unburnt.

While now we sang old songs that peal'd
    From knoll to knoll, where, couch'd at ease,[1]
    The white kine glimmer'd, and the trees   15
Laid their dark arms about the field.

But when those others, one by one,
    Withdrew themselves from me and night,[2]
    And in the house light after light
Went out, and I was all alone,   20

A hunger seized my heart; I read
    Of that glad year which once had been,
    In those fall'n leaves which kept their green,
The noble letters of the dead:

And strangely on the silence broke   25
    The silent-speaking words, and strange
    Was love's dumb cry defying change
To test his worth; and strangely spoke

The faith, the vigour, bold to dwell
    On doubts that drive the coward back,   30
    And keen thro' wordy snares to track
Suggestion to her inmost cell.

So word by word, and line by line,
    The dead man touch'd me from the past,
    And all at once it seem'd at last   35
The living soul[3] was flash'd on mine,

And mine in this was wound, and whirl'd
    About empyreal heights of thought,
    And came on that which is, and caught
The deep pulsations of the world,   40

---

1 Wordsworth, *The White Doe of Rylstone* (1836 and later editions) 1011–12: "the uncomplaining Doe / Now couched at ease."
2 Thomas Grey, "Elegy Written in a Country Churchyard" 4: "And leaves the world to darkness and to me."
3 "The Deity, maybe. The first reading ... troubled me, as perhaps giving a wrong impression" (T). In the first edition, and thereafter until 1870, these lines read "His living soul ... / And mine in his."

Æonian music measuring out
    The steps of Time—the shocks of Chance—
    The blows of Death.[1] At length my trance
Was cancell'd, stricken thro' with doubt.[2]

Vague words! But ah, how hard to frame   45
    In matter-moulded forms of speech,
    Or ev'n for intellect to reach
Thro' memory that which I became:

Till now the doubtful dusk reveal'd
    The knolls once more where, couch'd at ease,   50
    The white kine glimmer'd, and the trees
Laid their dark arms about the field:

And suck'd from out the distant gloom
    A breeze began to tremble o'er
    The large leaves of the sycamore,   55
And fluctuate all the still perfume,

And gathering freshlier overhead,
    Rock'd the full-foliaged elms, and swung
    The heavy-folded rose, and flung
The lilies to and fro, and said   60

"The dawn, the dawn," and died away;
    And East and West, without a breath,
    Mixt their dim lights, like life and death,
To broaden into boundless day.

XCVI.

You say, but with no touch of scorn,
    Sweet-hearted, you, whose light-blue eyes
    Are tender over drowning flies,
You tell me, doubt is Devil-born.

---

1 Milton, "On Time" 22: "Triumphing over Death, and Chance, and thee
    O Time."

2 "The trance came to an end in a moment of critical doubt, but the
    doubt was dispelled by the glory of the dawn of the 'boundless day'"
    (T). Compare the narration of Hallam's death in section 72.19–20: "the
    dark hand struck down through time, / And cancelled nature's best."

I know not: one indeed I knew   5
  In many a subtle question versed,
  Who touch'd a jarring lyre at first,
But ever strove to make it true:[1]

Perplext in faith, but pure in deeds,
  At last he beat his music out.   10
  There lives more faith in honest doubt,
Believe me, than in half the creeds.

He fought his doubts and gather'd strength,
  He would not make his judgment blind,
  He faced the spectres of the mind   15
And laid them: thus he came at length

To find a stronger faith his own;
  And Power was with him in the night,
  Which makes the darkness and the light,
And dwells not in the light alone,   20

But in the darkness and the cloud,
  As over Sinaï's peaks of old,
  While Israel made their gods of gold,
Altho' the trumpet blew so loud.[2]

XCVII.[3]

My love has talk'd with rocks and trees;
  He finds on misty mountain-ground
  His own vast shadow glory-crown'd;[4]
He sees himself in all he sees.

---

1 Hallam, as Tennyson notes. The contrast between the unquestioned faith
 of the female addressee and a man's struggle with doubt recalls the gen-
 dered representation of religious life elsewhere in the poem; see for
 instance section 33.

2 Tennyson notes the allusion to Exodus 19.16: "And it came to pass on
 the third day, in the morning, that there were thunders and lightnings,
 and a thick cloud upon the mount, and the voice of the trumpet exceed-
 ing loud."

3 "The relation of one on earth to one in the other and higher world. Not
 my relation to him here. He looked up to me as I looked up to him" (T).

4 "Like the spectre of the Brocken" (T). The spectre is an optical effect
 produced in mountainous country when the sun shining behind an
 observer casts his or her shadow on cloud or mist.

Two partners of a married life—   5
        I look'd on these and thought of thee
        In vastness and in mystery,
And of my spirit as of a wife.

These two—they dwelt with eye on eye,
        Their hearts of old have beat in tune,   10
        Their meetings made December June,
Their every parting was to die.

Their love has never past away;
        The days she never can forget
        Are earnest that he loves her yet,   15
Whate'er the faithless people say.

Her life is lone, he sits apart,
        He loves her yet, she will not weep,
        Tho' rapt in matters dark and deep
He seems to slight her simple heart.   20

He thrids¹ the labyrinth of the mind,
        He reads the secret of the star,
        He seems so near and yet so far,
He looks so cold: she thinks him kind.

She keeps the gift of years before,   25
        A wither'd violet is her bliss:
        She knows not what his greatness is,
For that, for all, she loves him more.

For him she plays, to him she sings
        Of early faith and plighted vows;   30
        She knows but matters of the house,
And he, he knows a thousand things.

Her faith is fixt and cannot move,
        She darkly feels him great and wise,
        She dwells on him with faithful eyes,   35
"I cannot understand: I love."

---

1   A variant spelling of threads.

XCVIII.

You leave us: you will see the Rhine,[1]
    And those fair hills I sail'd below,
    When I was there with him;[2] and go
By summer belts of wheat and vine

To where he breathed his latest breath,   5
    That City. All her splendour seems
    No livelier than the wisp that gleams
On Lethe[3] in the eyes of Death.

Let her great Danube rolling fair
    Enwind her isles, unmark'd of me: 10
    I have not seen, I will not see
Vienna; rather dream that there,

A treble darkness, Evil haunts
    The birth, the bridal; friend from friend
    Is oftener parted, fathers bend   15
Above more graves, a thousand wants

Gnarr[4] at the heels of men, and prey
    By each cold hearth, and sadness flings
    Her shadow on the blaze of kings:
And yet myself have heard him say,   20

That not in any mother town[5]
    With statelier progress to and fro
    The double tides of chariots flow
By park and suburb under brown

Of lustier leaves; nor more content,   25
    He told me, lives in any crowd,
    When all is gay with lamps, and loud
With sport and song, in booth and tent,

---

1 "'You' is imaginary" (T). The poem may actually have been prompted
    by the honeymoon of Tennyson's brother Charles on the Rhine in 1836.
2 Tennyson and Hallam toured the Rhine together in 1832.
3 In Greek mythology, Lethe was one of the five rivers of the underworld.
4 "Snarl" (T).
5 "Metropolis" (T).

Imperial halls, or open plain;
>   And wheels the circled dance, and breaks   30
>   The rocket molten into flakes
Of crimson or in emerald rain.

XCIX.

Risest thou thus, dim dawn, again,[1]
>   So loud with voices of the birds,
>   So thick with lowings of the herds,
Day, when I lost the flower of men;

Who tremblest thro' thy darkling red   5
>   On yon swoll'n brook that bubbles fast
>   By meadows breathing of the past,
And woodlands holy to the dead;

Who murmurest in the foliaged eaves
>   A song that slights the coming care,   10
>   And Autumn laying here and there
A fiery finger on the leaves;

Who wakenest with thy balmy breath[2]
>   To myriads on the genial earth,
>   Memories of bridal, or of birth,   15
And unto myriads more, of death.

O wheresoever those may be,
>   Betwixt the slumber of the poles,[3]
>   To-day they count as kindred souls;
They know me not, but mourn with me.   20

---

1   In the sequence's internal calendar, this section marks the second
     anniversary of Hallam's death on 15 September. It opens with an echo
     of section 72, which marked the first anniversary.

2   Shakespeare, *Othello* 5.2.16–17: "O balmy breath, that dost almost per-
     suade / Justice to break her sword!" As Ricks notes, the context includes
     both bridal and death.

3   "The ends of the axis of the earth, which move so slowly that they seem
     not to move, but slumber" (T).

C.[1]

I climb the hill: from end to end
    Of all the landscape underneath,
    I find no place that does not breathe
Some gracious memory of my friend;

No gray old grange, or lonely fold,   5
    Or low morass and whispering reed,
    Or simple stile from mead to mead,
Or sheepwalk up the windy wold;

Nor hoary knoll of ash and haw
    That hears the latest linnet trill,   10
    Nor quarry trench'd along the hill
And haunted by the wrangling daw;

Nor runlet tinkling from the rock;
    Nor pastoral rivulet that swerves
    To left and right thro' meadowy curves,   15
That feed the mothers of the flock;

But each has pleased a kindred eye,
    And each reflects a kindlier day;
    And, leaving these, to pass away,
I think once more he seems to die.   20

CI.

Unwatch'd, the garden bough shall sway,
    The tender blossom flutter down,
    Unloved, that beech will gather brown,
This maple burn itself away;

Unloved, the sun-flower, shining fair,   5
    Ray round with flames her disk of seed,
    And many a rose-carnation feed
With summer spice the humming air;

---

1 Sections 100–03 reflect the Tennyson family's move from Somersby in
1837. After Tennyson's father died in 1831 the family had been allowed
to remain in the rectory, but it was now needed for his successor. Ten-
nyson was born and grew up in the rectory; it also held memories of
Hallam, who visited there and became engaged to Emily Tennyson.

Unloved, by many a sandy bar,
　　The brook shall babble down the plain,   10
　　At noon or when the lesser wain
Is twisting round the polar star;[1]

Uncared for, gird the windy grove,
　　And flood the haunts of hern and crake;
　　Or into silver arrows break   15
The sailing moon in creek and cove;

Till from the garden and the wild[2]
　　A fresh association blow,
　　And year by year the landscape grow
Familiar to the stranger's child;   20

As year by year the labourer tills
　　His wonted glebe,[3] or lops the glades;
　　And year by year our memory fades
From all the circle of the hills.

CII.

We leave the well-beloved place
　　Where first we gazed upon the sky;
　　The roofs, that heard our earliest cry,
Will shelter one of stranger race.

We go, but ere we go from home,   5
　　As down the garden-walks I move,
　　Two spirits of a diverse love[4]
Contend for loving masterdom.

One whispers, "Here thy boyhood sung
　　Long since its matin song, and heard   10
　　The low love-language of the bird
In native hazels tassel-hung."

1　The constellation of *ursa minor*, which turns around the pole star.
2　Stanzas 1 and 2 describe the seasonal changes of the garden; stanzas 3
　　and 4 the unchanging course of the brook in the wild beyond it.
3　Field.
4　"First, the love of the native place; second, this enhanced by the
　　memory of A.H.H." (T). Compare Shakespeare, *Sonnets* 144.1–2: "Two
　　loves have I of comfort and despair, / Which like two spirits do suggest
　　me still."

The other answers, "Yea, but here
    Thy feet have stray'd in after hours
    With thy lost friend among the bowers,   15
And this hath made them trebly dear."

These two have striven half the day,
    And each prefers his separate claim,
    Poor rivals in a losing game,[1]
That will not yield each other way.   20

I turn to go: my feet are set
    To leave the pleasant fields and farms;
    They mix in one another's arms
To one pure image of regret.

CIII.

On that last night before we went
    From out the doors where I was bred,
    I dream'd a vision of the dead,
Which left my after-morn content.

Methought I dwelt within a hall,   5
    And maidens with me:[2] distant hills
    From hidden summits fed with rills
A river sliding by the wall.

The hall with harp and carol rang.
    They sang of what is wise and good   10
    And graceful. In the centre stood
A statue veil'd, to which they sang;

And which, tho' veil'd, was known to me,
    The shape of him I loved, and love
    For ever: then flew in a dove   15
And brought a summons from the sea:

And when they learnt that I must go
    They wept and wail'd, but led the way
    To where a little shallop lay
At anchor in the flood below;   20

---

1 A losing game is one in which the loser of the game wins the stakes.
2 "They are the Muses, poetry, arts—all that made life beautiful here,
    which we hope will pass with us beyond the grave" (T).

And on by many a level mead,
    And shadowing bluff that made the banks,
    We glided winding under ranks
Of iris, and the golden reed;

And still as vaster grew the shore   25
    And roll'd the floods in grander space,
    The maidens gather'd strength and grace
And presence, lordlier than before;[1]

And I myself, who sat apart
    And watch'd them, wax'd in every limb;   30
    I felt the thews of Anakim,
The pulses of a Titan's heart;[2]

As one would sing the death of war,
    And one would chant the history
    Of that great race, which is to be,   35
And one the shaping of a star;

Until the forward-creeping tides
    Began to foam, and we to draw
    From deep to deep, to where we saw
A great ship lift her shining sides.   40

The man we loved was there on deck,
    But thrice as large as man he bent
    To greet us.[3] Up the side I went,
And fell in silence on his neck:

Whereat those maidens with one mind   45
    Bewail'd their lot; I did them wrong:
    "We served thee here," they said, "so long,
And wilt thou leave us now behind?"

So rapt I was, they could not win
    An answer from my lips, but he   50

---

1 "The progress of the age" (T).
2 Anakim are giants in Deuteronomy 2.10–11; in Greek mythology the
    Titans were a giant race of gods who preceded the gods of Olympus.
3 See Shatto and Shaw 263–64 for the idea that ghosts are larger than
    living mortals in Latin literature and in Tennyson's writing elsewhere.

Replying, "Enter likewise ye
And go with us:" they enter'd in.

And while the wind began to sweep
    A music out of sheet and shroud,
    We steer'd her toward a crimson cloud   55
That landlike slept along the deep.

CIV.[1]

The time draws near the birth of Christ;
    The moon is hid, the night is still;
    A single church below the hill
Is pealing, folded in the mist.

A single peal of bells below,   5
    That wakens at this hour of rest
    A single murmur in the breast,
That these are not the bells I know.

Like strangers' voices here they sound,
    In lands where not a memory strays,   10
    Nor landmark breathes of other days,
But all is new unhallow'd ground.[2]

CV.

To-night ungather'd let us leave
    This laurel, let this holly stand:
    We live within the stranger's land,
And strangely falls our Christmas-eve.

Our father's dust is left alone   5
    And silent under other snows:[3]
    There in due time the woodbine blows,
The violet comes, but we are gone.

No more shall wayward grief abuse
    The genial hour with mask and mime;   10

---

1 In sections 104 and 105 the poem marks the approach of the third
    Christmas after Hallam's death; the family has moved to a new home.
    For the first and second Christmases, see sections 28–30 and 78.
2 "High Beech, Epping Forest (where we were living)" (T).
3 Tennyson's father is buried in the churchyard at Somersby.

For change of place, like growth of time,
Has broke the bond of dying use.

Let cares that petty shadows cast,
 By which our lives are chiefly proved,
 A little spare the night I loved,   15
And hold it solemn to the past.

But let no footstep beat the floor,
 Nor bowl of wassail mantle warm;
 For who would keep an ancient form
Thro' which the spirit breathes no more?   20

Be neither song, nor game, nor feast;
 Nor harp be touch'd, nor flute be blown;
 No dance, no motion, save alone
What lightens in the lucid east

Of rising worlds by yonder wood.   25
 Long sleeps the summer in the seed;
 Run out your measured arcs, and lead
The closing cycle rich in good.[1]

CVI.[2]

Ring out, wild bells, to the wild sky,
 The flying cloud, the frosty light:
 The year is dying in the night;
Ring out, wild bells, and let him die.

Ring out the old, ring in the new,   5
 Ring, happy bells, across the snow:
 The year is going, let him go;
Ring out the false, ring in the true.

Ring out the grief that saps the mind,
 For those that here we see no more;   10

---

1 Hallam Tennyson cites Virgil, *Eclogues* 4; see 4–5: "Ultima Cumaei venit
 iam carminis aetas; / magnus ab integro saeclorum nascitur ordo [Now
 is come the last age of the song of Cumae: the great line of the centuries
 begins anew]." On cyclical time in the Roman poets, see A.C. Bradley's
 note to this line.
2 New Year's Eve.

Ring out the feud of rich and poor,
Ring in redress to all mankind.

Ring out a slowly dying cause,
  And ancient forms of party strife;
  Ring in the nobler modes of life,   15
With sweeter manners, purer laws.

Ring out the want, the care, the sin,
  The faithless coldness of the times;
  Ring out, ring out my mournful rhymes,
But ring the fuller minstrel in.   20

Ring out false pride in place and blood,
  The civic slander and the spite;
  Ring in the love of truth and right,
Ring in the common love of good.

Ring out old shapes of foul disease;   25
  Ring out the narrowing lust of gold;
  Ring out the thousand wars of old,
Ring in the thousand years of peace.

Ring in the valiant man and free,
  The larger heart, the kindlier hand;   30
  Ring out the darkness of the land,
Ring in the Christ that is to be.[1]

CVII.[2]

It is the day when he was born,[3]
  A bitter day that early sank
  Behind a purple-frosty bank
Of vapour, leaving night forlorn.

The time admits not flowers or leaves   5
  To deck the banquet. Fiercely flies
  The blast of North and East, and ice
Makes daggers at the sharpen'd eaves,

---

1 "The broader Christianity of the future" (T).
2 This section adapts Alcaeus fragment 338 and Horace *Odes* 1.9; for the
 relevant passages see Shatto and Shaw 266–67.
3 "February 1, 1811" (T).

And bristles all the brakes and thorns
    To yon hard crescent, as she hangs   10
    Above the wood which grides[1] and clangs
Its leafless ribs and iron horns

Together, in the drifts that pass
    To darken on the rolling brine
    That breaks the coast. But fetch the wine,   15
Arrange the board and brim the glass;

Bring in great logs and let them lie,
    To make a solid core of heat;
    Be cheerful-minded, talk and treat
Of all things ev'n as he were by;   20

We keep the day. With festal cheer,
    With books and music, surely we
    Will drink to him, whate'er he be,
And sing the songs he loved to hear.

CVIII.[2]

I will not shut me from my kind,
    And, lest I stiffen into stone,
    I will not eat my heart alone,
Nor feed with sighs a passing wind:

What profit lies in barren faith,   5
    And vacant yearning, tho' with might
    To scale the heaven's highest height,
Or dive below the wells of Death?[3]

---

1 "Grates" (T).

2 "Grief shall not make me a hermit, and I will not indulge in vacant
    yearnings and barren aspirations; it is useless trying to find him in other
    worlds—I find nothing but the reflections of myself: I had better learn
    the lesson that sorrow teaches" (T).

3 Ricks notes an allusion to Romans 10.6–7: "Say not in thine heart, Who
    shall ascend into heaven? (that is, to bring Christ down *from above*:), or,
    Who shall descend into the deep? (that is, to bring Christ up again from
    the dead.)"

What find I in the highest place,
        But mine own phantom chanting hymns?   10
        And on the depths of death there swims
The reflex of a human face.

I'll rather take what fruit may be
        Of sorrow under human skies:
        'Tis held that sorrow makes us wise,   15
Whatever wisdom sleep with thee.

CIX.

Heart-affluence in discursive talk
        From household fountains never dry;
        The critic clearness of an eye,
That saw thro' all the Muses' walk;

Seraphic intellect and force   5
        To seize and throw the doubts of man;
        Impassion'd logic, which outran
The hearer in its fiery course;

High nature amorous of the good,
        But touch'd with no ascetic gloom;   10
        And passion pure in snowy bloom
Thro' all the years of April blood;

A love of freedom rarely felt,
        Of freedom in her regal seat
        Of England; not the schoolboy heat,   15
The blind hysterics of the Celt;

And manhood fused with female grace
        In such a sort, the child would twine
        A trustful hand, unask'd, in thine,
And find his comfort in thy face;   20

All these have been, and thee mine eyes
        Have look'd on: if they look'd in vain,
        My shame is greater who remain,
Nor let thy wisdom make me wise.[1]

---

1   "If I do not let thy wisdom make me wise" (T).

CX.

Thy converse drew us with delight,
    The men of rathe[1] and riper years:
    The feeble soul, a haunt of fears,
Forgot his weakness in thy sight.

On thee the loyal-hearted hung,   5
    The proud was half disarm'd of pride,
    Nor cared the serpent at thy side
To flicker with his double tongue.

The stern were mild when thou wert by,
    The flippant put himself to school   10
    And heard thee, and the brazen fool
Was soften'd, and he knew not why;

While I, thy nearest,[2] sat apart,
    And felt thy triumph was as mine;
    And loved them more, that they were thine,   15
The graceful tact, the Christian art;

Nor mine the sweetness or the skill,
    But mine the love that will not tire,
    And, born of love, the vague desire
That spurs an imitative will.   20

CXI.

The churl in spirit, up or down
    Along the scale of ranks, thro' all,
    To him who grasps a golden ball,[3]
By blood a king, at heart a clown;

The churl in spirit, howe'er he veil   5
    His want in forms for fashion's sake,
    Will let his coltish nature break
At seasons thro' the gilded pale:

---

1 Early.
2 From the first edition until 1874, this read "dearest."
3 A churl is a serf; "him who grasps the golden ball" is the king. England
    did not have serfs in 1850, or a king, and the language of class in this
    section is typically Victorian in its recourse to anachronism and cliché.

For who can always act? But he,
    To whom a thousand memories call,   10
    Not being less but more than all
The gentleness he seem'd to be,

Best seem'd the thing he was, and join'd
    Each office of the social hour
    To noble manners, as the flower   15
And native growth of noble mind;

Nor ever narrowness or spite,
    Or villain fancy fleeting by,
    Drew in the expression of an eye,
Where God and Nature met in light;   20

And thus he bore without abuse
    The grand old name of gentleman,[1]
    Defamed by every charlatan,[2]
And soil'd with all ignoble use.

CXII.

High wisdom holds my wisdom less,[3]
    That I, who gaze with temperate eyes
    On glorious insufficiencies,[4]
Set light by narrower perfectness.

But thou, that fillest all the room   5
    Of all my love, art reason why

---

1   A review by Franklin Lushington in *Tait's Edinburgh Magazine* (August
    1850) saw here an allusion to a song, presumably Henry Russell's "The
    Fine Old English Gentleman" (1836). Lushington wrote "The 'grand
    old name of gentleman'" has been "'soiled with all ignoble use' of the-
    atrical and other parodies of the original 'good old song' ... till, we fear,
    nothing can be done to retrieve its character." Quoted Shatto and Shaw
    269.
2   "From Ital. *ciarlatino*, a mountebank; hence the accent on the last sylla-
    ble" (T).
3   Hallam Tennyson notes: "*High wisdom* is ironical. 'High wisdom' has
    been twitting the poet that although he gazes with calm and indulgent
    eyes on unaccomplished greatness, yet he makes light of narrower
    natures more perfect in their own small way."
4   "Unaccomplished greatness such as Arthur Hallam's" (T).

I seem to cast a careless eye
On souls, the lesser lords of doom.[1]

For what wert thou? Some novel power
    Sprang up for ever at a touch,   10
    And hope could never hope too much,
In watching thee from hour to hour,

Large elements in order brought,
    And tracts of calm from tempest made,
    And world-wide fluctuation sway'd   15
In vassal tides that follow'd thought.

CXIII.

'Tis held that sorrow makes us wise;
    Yet how much wisdom sleeps with thee
    Which not alone had guided me,
But served the seasons that may rise;

For can I doubt, who knew thee keen   5
    In intellect, with force and skill
    To strive, to fashion, to fulfil—
I doubt not what thou wouldst have been:

A life in civic action warm,
    A soul on highest mission sent,   10
    A potent voice of Parliament,[2]
A pillar steadfast in the storm,

Should licensed boldness gather force,
    Becoming, when the time has birth,
    A lever to uplift the earth   15
And roll it in another course,

With thousand shocks that come and go,
    With agonies, with energies,
    With overthrowings, and with cries,
And undulations to and fro.   20

---

1   "Those that have free-will, but less intellect" (T).
2   Milton, *Paradise Lost* 7.100: "thy potent voice he hears."

CXIV.

Who loves not Knowledge? Who shall rail
    Against her beauty? May she mix
    With men and prosper! Who shall fix
Her pillars?[1] Let her work prevail.

But on her forehead sits a fire: 5
    She sets her forward countenance
    And leaps into the future chance,
Submitting all things to desire.

Half-grown as yet, a child, and vain—
    She cannot fight the fear of death.   10
    What is she, cut from love and faith,
But some wild Pallas from the brain

Of Demons?[2] fiery-hot to burst
    All barriers in her onward race
    For power. Let her know her place: 15
She is the second, not the first.

A higher hand must make her mild,
    If all be not in vain; and guide
    Her footsteps, moving side by side
With wisdom, like the younger child: 20

For she is earthly of the mind,
    But Wisdom heavenly of the soul.
    O, friend, who camest to thy goal
So early, leaving me behind,[3]

I would the great world grew like thee,   25
    Who grewest not alone in power
    And knowledge, but by year and hour
In reverence and in charity.

---

1 Tennyson cites Proverbs 9.1: "Wisdom hath builded her house, she hath
    hewn out her seven pillars."

2 An allusion to the myth of Pallas Athena's birth full-grown from the
    brain of Zeus.

3 For early death as victory in a race, see Dryden, "To the Memory of
    Mr. Oldham" 7–10.

CXV.

Now fades the last long streak of snow,
    Now burgeons every maze of quick[1]
    About the flowering squares, and thick
By ashen roots the violets blow.

Now rings the woodland loud and long,   5
    The distance takes a lovelier hue,
    And drown'd in yonder living blue
The lark becomes a sightless song.[2]

Now dance the lights on lawn and lea,
    The flocks are whiter down the vale,   10
    And milkier every milky sail
On winding stream or distant sea;

Where now the seamew pipes, or dives
    In yonder greening gleam, and fly
    The happy birds, that change their sky   15
To build and brood; that live their lives

From land to land; and in my breast
    Spring wakens too; and my regret
    Becomes an April violet,
And buds and blossoms like the rest.

CXVI.

Is it, then, regret for buried time
    That keenlier in sweet April wakes,
    And meets the year, and gives and takes
The colours of the crescent prime?[3]

Not all: the songs, the stirring air,   5
    The life re-orient out of dust,
    Cry thro' the sense to hearten trust
In that which made the world so fair.

---

1 "Burgeons" means "buds." The maze of quick is the tangle of a flower-
    ing hedge.

2 "Sightless" means "invisible." With this image, compare Shelley, "To a
    Skylark."

3 "Growing spring" (T). As in section 83, Tennyson sets the new year in
    spring.

Not all regret: the face will shine
    Upon me, while I muse alone;   10
    And that dear voice, I once have known,
Still speak to me of me and mine:

Yet less of sorrow lives in me
    For days of happy commune dead;
    Less yearning for the friendship fled,   15
Than some strong bond which is to be.

CXVII.

O days and hours, your work is this
    To hold me from my proper place,
    A little while from his embrace,
For fuller gain of after bliss:

That out of distance might ensue   5
    Desire of nearness doubly sweet;
    And unto meeting when we meet,
Delight a hundredfold accrue,

For every grain of sand that runs,
    And every span of shade that steals,[1]   10
    And every kiss of toothed wheels,[2]
And all the courses of the suns.

CXVIII.

Contemplate all this work of Time,
    The giant labouring in his youth;
    Nor dream of human love and truth,
As dying Nature's earth and lime;[3]

But trust that those we call the dead   5
    Are breathers of an ampler day[4]
    For ever nobler ends. They say,
The solid earth whereon we tread

---

1 "The sun-dial" (T).
2 "The clock" (T).
3 Earth and lime are flesh and bone. In Genesis 2, God made Adam from the earth; in Amos 2.1 he "burned to lime the bones of the king of Edom."
4 In Virgil, *Aeneid* 6.640 the dead in Elysium breathe an "ampler air [largior ... aether]."

In tracts of fluent heat began,
  And grew to seeming-random forms,
  The seeming prey of cyclic storms,[1]
Till at the last arose the man;   10

Who throve and branch'd from clime to clime,[2]
  The herald of a higher race,
  And of himself in higher place,
If so he type this work of time[3]   15

Within himself, from more to more;
  Or, crown'd with attributes of woe
  Like glories, move his course, and show
That life is not as idle ore,   20

But iron dug from central gloom,
  And heated hot with burning fears,
  And dipt in baths of hissing tears,
And batter'd with the shocks of doom

To shape and use. Arise and fly   25
  The reeling Faun,[4] the sensual feast;[5]
  Move upward, working out the beast,
And let the ape and tiger die.[6]

---

1 The theory that species extinctions in the past were caused by periodic
   global catastrophes.
2 Ricks cites Robert Chambers, *Vestiges of Creation* 262: "It may only have
   been when a varied climate arose, that the originally few species
   branched off into the present extensive variety."
3 "Type" here could mean to reproduce the work of time within himself,
   or to anticipate its work in the future.
4 A figure from Greek and Latin literature, half-human and half-goat,
   here used to symbolize drunkenness and sexual license.
5 Shakespeare, *Sonnets* 141.7–8: "to be invited / To any sensual feast."
6 The language of extinction here is used primarily to symbolize the sup-
   pression of "beastly" traits in individuals. The ape and the tiger,
   however, often appeared in late Victorian racist texts to represent the
   supposed African and Asian races.

CXIX.[1]

Doors, where my heart was used to beat
    So quickly, not as one that weeps
    I come once more; the city sleeps;
I smell the meadow in the street;

I hear a chirp of birds; I see   5
    Betwixt the black fronts long-withdrawn
    A light-blue lane of early dawn,
And think of early days and thee,

And bless thee, for thy lips are bland,
    And bright the friendship of thine eye;   10
    And in my thoughts with scarce a sigh
I take the pressure of thine hand.

CXX.

I trust I have not wasted breath:
    I think we are not wholly brain,
    Magnetic mockeries; not in vain,
Like Paul with beasts, I fought with Death;[2]

Not only cunning casts in clay: 5
    Let Science prove we are, and then
    What matters Science unto men,
At least to me? I would not stay.

Let him, the wiser man who springs
    Hereafter, up from childhood shape   10
    His action like the greater ape,[3]
But I was *born* to other things.

---

1 This section returns to the situation of section 7, which it echoes
    throughout.

2 Tennyson cites 1 Corinthians 15.32: "If after the manner of men I have
    fought with beasts at Ephesus, what advantageth it me, if the dead rise
    not? Let us eat and drink; for tomorrow we die."

3 "Spoken ironically against mere materialism, not against evolution"
    (T).

CXXI.[1]

Sad Hesper o'er the buried sun
    And ready, thou, to die with him,
    Thou watchest all things ever dim
And dimmer, and a glory done:

The team is loosen'd from the wain,   5
    The boat is drawn upon the shore;
    Thou listenest to the closing door,
And life is darken'd in the brain.

Bright Phosphor, fresher for the night,
    By thee the world's great work is heard   10
    Beginning, and the wakeful bird;[2]
Behind thee comes the greater light:[3]

The market boat is on the stream,
    And voices hail it from the brink;
    Thou hear'st the village hammer clink,   15
And see'st the moving of the team.

Sweet Hesper-Phosphor, double name
    For what is one, the first, the last,[4]
    Thou, like my present and my past,
Thy place is changed; thou art the same.   20

---

1 A.C. Bradley comments on this section: "Hesper, the evening star, which follows the setting sun and watches the fading light and ending life of day, is also Phosphor, the morning-star, which precedes the sun and sees the dawn of light and life." Both the evening star and the morning star are the planet Venus, shining by the sun's reflected light; they are both, as Bradley says, "the same 'planet of love' ... which does but change its place. And so the poet's past and present are in substance one thing (Love), which has merely changed its place in becoming present instead of past" (218). One source for the section is an epigram attributed to Plato; as Shatto and Shaw note, Shelley used it as the epigraph to "Adonais" and elsewhere translated it: "Thou wert the morning star among the living, / Ere thy fair light had fled;— / Now, having died, thou art as Hesperus, giving / Light among the dead."

2 Milton *Paradise Lost* 3.38–39: "the wakeful bird / Sings darkling."

3 Genesis 1.16: "the greater light to rule the day."

4 Revelations 22.13: "I am the Alpha and the Omega, the beginning and the end, the first and the last."

CXXII.

Oh, wast thou with me, dearest, then,[1]
    While I rose up against my doom,
    And yearn'd to burst the folded gloom,
To bare the eternal Heavens again,

To feel once more, in placid awe,   5
    The strong imagination roll
    A sphere of stars about my soul,
In all her motion one with law;[2]

If thou wert with me, and the grave
    Divide us not, be with me now,   10
    And enter in at breast and brow,
Till all my blood, a fuller wave,

Be quicken'd with a livelier breath,
    And like an inconsiderate boy,
    As in the former flash of joy,   15
I slip the thoughts of life and death;

And all the breeze of Fancy blows,
    And every dew-drop paints a bow,
    The wizard lightnings deeply glow,
And every thought breaks out a rose.   20

CXXIII.

There rolls the deep where grew the tree.[3]
    O earth, what changes hast thou seen!
    There where the long street roars, hath been
The stillness of the central sea.

---

1 Tennyson said to James Knowles: "If anybody thinks I ever called him 'dearest' in his life they are much mistaken, for I never even called him 'dear'" (Knowles 187).

2 The first two stanzas of this section refer to a time when the speaker "rose up" and "yearned to feel once more ... the strong imagination." It seems likely that the time referred to was that of section 95; nothing in that section, though, implies that it repeats an earlier experience, while the words "once more" do make that implication here. For a statement of the problem and a survey of possible solutions, see A.C. Bradley 219–26.

3 Compare Charles Lyell's description of subsidence from *Principles of Geology* in Appendix B2 (p. 164).

The hills are shadows, and they flow[1]   5
    From form to form, and nothing stands;
    They melt like mist, the solid lands,
Like clouds they shape themselves and go.[2]

But in my spirit will I dwell,
    And dream my dream, and hold it true;   10
    For tho' my lips may breathe adieu,
I cannot think the thing farewell.

CXXIV.

That which we dare invoke to bless;
    Our dearest faith; our ghastliest doubt;
    He, They, One, All; within, without;
The Power in darkness whom we guess;

I found Him not in world or sun,   5
    Or eagle's wing, or insect's eye;[3]
    Nor thro' the questions men may try,
The petty cobwebs we have spun:

If e'er when faith had fall'n asleep,
    I heard a voice "believe no more"   10
    And heard an ever-breaking shore
That tumbled in the Godless deep;

A warmth within the breast would melt
    The freezing reason's colder part,
    And like a man in wrath the heart   15
Stood up and answer'd "I have felt."

No, like a child in doubt and fear:
    But that blind clamour made me wise;

---

1 Shatto and Shaw cite Isaiah 64.3: "the mountains flowed down at thy presence."

2 Ricks cites Wordsworth, *The White Doe of Rylstone* 969–70 "A thousand, thousand rings of light / That shape themselves and disappear."

3 Here Tennyson rejects the argument that God's existence can be inferred by observation of the natural world, commonly termed the argument from design. For the most influential statement of this argument, probably referred to in these lines, see the extract from William Paley's *Natural Theology* in Appendix B1 (p. 157).

Then was I as a child that cries
But, crying, knows his father near;[1]   20

And what I am beheld again
    What is, and no man understands;[2]
    And out of darkness came the hands
That reach thro' nature, moulding men.[3]

CXXV.

Whatever I have said or sung,
    Some bitter notes my harp would give,
    Yea, tho' there often seem'd to live
A contradiction on the tongue,

Yet Hope had never lost her youth;   5
    She did but look through dimmer eyes;
    Or Love but play'd with gracious lies,
Because he felt so fix'd in truth:

And if the song were full of care,
    He breathed the spirit of the song;   10
    And if the words were sweet and strong
He set his royal signet there;

Abiding with me till I sail
    To seek thee on the mystic deeps,
    And this electric force that keeps   15
A thousand pulses dancing, fail.

CXXVI.

Love is and was my Lord and King,
    And in his presence I attend
    To hear the tidings of my friend,
Which every hour his couriers bring.

---

1 A recollection and reinterpretation of the speaker's self-representation in
   section 54.
2 In manuscript and in the trial edition, l.21–22 read "And the inner eye
   beheld again / The form which no one understands." In the first edition,
   the lines stood as at present, except that instead of "what I am" Ten-
   nyson wrote "what I seem." He adopted the final wording in 1859.
3 The last of a series of hand images in the poem that began in section 1.

Love is and was my King and Lord,   5
        And will be, tho' as yet I keep
        Within his court on earth, and sleep
Encompass'd by his faithful guard,

And hear at times a sentinel
        Who moves about from place to place,   10
        And whispers to the worlds of space,
In the deep night, that all is well.

CXXVII.

And all is well, tho' faith and form
        Be sunder'd in the night of fear;
        Well roars the storm to those that hear
A deeper voice across the storm,

Proclaiming social truth shall spread,   5
        And justice, ev'n tho thrice again
        The red fool-fury of the Seine
Should pile her barricades with dead.[1]

But ill for him that wears a crown,
        And him, the lazar,[2] in his rags: 10
        They tremble, the sustaining crags;
The spires of ice are toppled down,[3]

And molten up, and roar in flood;
        The fortress crashes from on high,
        The brute earth lightens to the sky,[4]   15
And the great Æon sinks in blood,

---

1 Refers to the three revolutionary years in France: 1789, 1830, and 1848.
2 Archaic word for leper.
3 Shelley, *Prometheus Unbound* 2.3.28–30: "And far on high the keen sky-cleaving mountains / From icy spires of sunlike radiance fling / The dawn." The context is a comparison of a morning avalanche to political revolution.
4 Milton, *Comus* 797–99: "And the brute earth would lend her nerves, and shake, / Till all thy magic structures reared so high, / Were shattered into heaps."

And compass'd by the fires of Hell;
    While thou, dear spirit, happy star,[1]
    O'erlook'st the tumult from afar,
And smilest, knowing all is well.

CXXVIII.

The love that rose on stronger wings,
    Unpalsied when he met with Death,
    Is comrade of the lesser faith
That sees the course of human things.

No doubt vast eddies in the flood   5
    Of onward time shall yet be made,
    And throned races may degrade;
Yet O ye mysteries of good,

Wild Hours that fly with Hope and Fear,
    If all your office had to do   10
    With old results that look like new;
If this were all your mission here,

To draw, to sheathe a useless sword,
    To fool the crowd with glorious lies,
    To cleave a creed in sects and cries,   15
To change the bearing of a word,

To shift an arbitrary power,
    To cramp the student at his desk,
    To make old bareness picturesque
And tuft with grass a feudal tower;   20

Why then my scorn might well descend
    On you and yours. I see in part[2]
    That all, as in some piece of art,
Is toil cöoperant to an end.

---

1 The final appearance of the dead friend in the heavens as a star is a con-
    vention of elegy followed by Milton in "Lycidas" (167–73) and Shelley
    in "Adonais" (494–95).
2 1 Corinthians 13.12: "For now we see through a glass, darkly; but then
    face to face: now I know in part; but then shall I know even as I am
    known."

CXXIX.

Dear friend, far off, my lost desire,
    So far, so near in woe and weal;
    O loved the most, when most I feel
There is a lower and a higher;

Known and unknown; human, divine;   5
    Sweet human hand and lips and eye;
    Dear heavenly friend that canst not die,
Mine, mine, for ever, ever mine;

Strange friend, past, present, and to be;
    Loved deeplier, darklier understood;   10
    Behold, I dream a dream of good,
And mingle all the world with thee.

CXXX.

Thy voice is on the rolling air;
    I hear thee where the waters run;
    Thou standest in the rising sun,[1]
And in the setting thou art fair.

What art thou then? I cannot guess;   5
    But tho' I seem in star and flower
    To feel thee some diffusive power,
I do not therefore love thee less:

My love involves[2] the love before;
    My love is vaster passion now;   10
    Tho' mix'd with God and Nature thou,[3]
I seem to love thee more and more.

Far off thou art, but ever nigh;
    I have thee still, and I rejoice;
    I prosper, circled with thy voice;   15
I shall not lose thee tho' I die.

---

1 Revelations 19.17: "And I saw an angel standing in the sun." Also *Paradise Lost* 3.622–23: "And saw within ken a glorious angel stand, / The same whom John saw also in the sun."
2 "Involve" literally means "to enfold."
3 Compare Shelley's "Adonais" 370–87, where the dead friend "is made one with Nature: there is heard / His voice in all her music."

CXXXI.

O living will that shalt endure[1]
    When all that seems shall suffer shock,
    Rise in the spiritual rock,[2]
Flow thro' our deeds and make them pure,

That we may lift from out of dust[3]   5
    A voice as unto him that hears,
    A cry above the conquer'd years
To one that with us works, and trust,[4]

With faith that comes of self-control,
    The truths that never can be proved   10
    Until we close with all we loved,
And all we flow from, soul in soul.

––––––––

1 "That which we know as Free-will in man" (T).
2 1 Corinthians 10.4: "they drank of that spiritual Rock that followed
    them: and that Rock was Christ." This New Testament passage refers to
    one from the Old Testament, Exodus 17.6, where God commands
    Moses to obtain water for his people in the wilderness by striking a
    rock.
3 Isaiah 29.4: "And thou shalt be brought down, and shalt speak out of
    the ground, and thy speech shall be low out of the dust."
4 Mark 16.20: "And they went forth, and preached every where, the Lord
    working with them."

O true and tried, so well and long,[1]
    Demand not thou a marriage lay;[2]
    In that it is thy marriage day
Is music more than any song.

Nor have I felt so much of bliss   5
    Since first he told me that he loved
    A daughter of our house; nor proved
Since that dark day a day like this;

Tho' I since then have number'd o'er
    Some thrice three years:[3] they went and came,   10
    Remade the blood and changed the frame,
And yet is love not less, but more;

No longer caring to embalm
    In dying songs a dead regret,
    But like a statue solid-set,   15
And moulded in colossal calm.

Regret is dead, but love is more
    Than in the summers that are flown,
    For I myself with these have grown
To something greater than before;   20

Which makes appear the songs I made
    As echoes out of weaker times,
    As half but idle brawling rhymes,
The sport of random sun and shade.[4]

---

1 This address to Edmund Lushington echoes that in section 85.5. This
    final section of the poem celebrates Lushington's wedding to Tennyson's
    sister Cecilia. The wedding took place at Boxley Church, near Maid-
    stone, Kent in October 1842.

2 "Lay" means "song"; from the Old French *lai*.

3 It is nine years since Hallam's death; this epithalamium thus views the
    three-year calendar of the sequence's numbered sections in retrospect.

4 This half-retraction, later in the sequence but earlier in time, anticipates
    the retraction to be found at the end of the unnumbered first section.

But where is she, the bridal flower,   25
    That must be made a wife ere noon?[1]
    She enters, glowing like the moon
Of Eden on its bridal bower:

On me she bends her blissful eyes
    And then on thee; they meet thy look   30
    And brighten like the star that shook
Betwixt the palms of paradise.

O when her life was yet in bud,
    He too foretold the perfect rose.
    For thee she grew, for thee she grows   35
For ever, and as fair as good.

And thou art worthy; full of power;
    As gentle; liberal-minded, great,
    Consistent; wearing all that weight
Of learning lightly like a flower.   40

But now set out: the noon is near,
    And I must give away the bride;[2]
    She fears not, or with thee beside
And me behind her, will not fear.

For I that danced her on my knee,   45
    That watch'd her on her nurse's arm,
    That shielded all her life from harm
At last must part with her to thee;

Now waiting to be made a wife,
    Her feet, my darling, on the dead   50
    Their pensive tablets round her head,[3]
And the most living words of life

Breathed in her ear. The ring is on,
    The "wilt thou" answer'd, and again

---

1 Canon law in England required that weddings be held between eight
    a.m. and noon.
2 Dr. Tennyson, Alfred and Cecilia's father, had died in 1831.
3 In Boxley Church, as in most English parish churches, there are graves
    under the aisle and commemorative tablets on the walls.

The "wilt thou" ask'd, till out of twain   55
Her sweet "I will" has made you one.

Now sign your names, which shall be read,
        Mute symbols of a joyful morn,
        By village eyes as yet unborn;
The names are sign'd, and overhead   60

Begins the clash and clang that tells
        The joy to every wandering breeze;
        The blind wall rocks, and on the trees
The dead leaf trembles to the bells.

O happy hour, and happier hours   65
        Await them. Many a merry face
        Salutes them—maidens of the place,
That pelt us in the porch with flowers.

O happy hour, behold the bride
        With him to whom her hand I gave.   70
        They leave the porch, they pass the grave
That has to-day its sunny side.

To-day the grave is bright for me,
        For them the light of life increased,
        Who stay to share the morning feast,   75
Who rest to-night beside the sea.

Let all my genial spirits advance[1]
        To meet and greet a whiter sun;
        My drooping memory will not shun
The foaming grape of eastern France.[2]   80

It circles round, and fancy plays,
        And hearts are warm'd and faces bloom,
        As drinking health to bride and groom
We wish them store of happy days.

Nor count me all to blame if I   85
        Conjecture of a stiller guest,

---

1   Milton, *Samson Agonistes* 594: "my genial spirits droop."
2   Tennysonian periphrasis for champagne.

Perchance, perchance, among the rest,
And, tho' in silence, wishing joy.

But they must go, the time draws on,
    And those white-favour'd[1] horses wait;   90
    They rise, but linger; it is late;
Farewell, we kiss, and they are gone.

A shade falls on us like the dark
    From little cloudlets on the grass,
    But sweeps away as out we pass   95
To range the woods, to roam the park,

Discussing how their courtship grew,
    And talk of others that are wed,
    And how she look'd, and what he said,
And back we come at fall of dew.   100

Again the feast, the speech, the glee,
    The shade of passing thought, the wealth
    Of words and wit, the double health,
The crowning cup, the three-times-three,

And last the dance;—till I retire: 105
    Dumb is that tower which spake so loud,
    And high in heaven the streaming cloud,
And on the downs a rising fire:

And rise, O moon, from yonder down,
    Till over down and over dale   110
    All night the shining vapour sail
And pass the silent-lighted town,

The white-faced halls, the glancing rills,
    And catch at every mountain head,
    And o'er the friths[2] that branch and spread   115
Their sleeping silver thro' the hills;

---

1   A "favour" is a ribbon or rosette.
2   Frith is an archaic spelling of firth, i.e. a river estuary or arm of the sea.

And touch with shade the bridal doors,
  With tender gloom the roof, the wall;
  And breaking let the splendour fall
To spangle all the happy shores   120

By which they rest, and ocean sounds,
  And, star and system rolling past,
  A soul shall draw from out the vast
And strike his being into bounds,

And, moved thro' life of lower phase,[1]   125
  Result in man, be born and think,
  And act and love, a closer link
Betwixt us and the crowning race[2]

Of those that, eye to eye, shall look
  On knowledge; under whose command   130
  Is Earth and Earth's, and in their hand
Is Nature like an open book;

No longer half-akin to brute,
  For all we thought and loved and did,
  And hoped, and suffer'd, is but seed   135
Of what in them is flower and fruit;

Whereof the man, that with me trod
  This planet, was a noble type[3]
  Appearing ere the times were ripe,[4]
That friend of mine who lives in God,   140

That God, which ever lives and loves,
  One God, one law, one element,
  And one far-off divine event,
To which the whole creation moves.

---

1 A reference to the theory, developed by Karl Von Baer and generally
   accepted in the nineteenth century, that the development of the individ-
   ual embryo recapitulates the evolution of the species.
2 Tennyson recalls Robert Chambers's question in *Vestiges of Creation*: "Is
   our race but the initial of the grand crowning type?" See Appendix B3
   (p. 168).
3 The word "type" here primarily means "prefiguration," but it recalls the
   many uses of the term in other senses earlier in the poem.
4 Shakespeare *1 Henry IV* 1.3.294: "When time is ripe, which will be
   suddenly."

Appendix A: Writings of Arthur Hallam

[Arthur Hallam (1811–33) is today best known for his friendships, the most celebrated of which were with the future prime minister W.E. Gladstone while they were at boarding school at Eton, and with Alfred Tennyson, with whom he studied at Cambridge. Hallam and Tennyson were both members of the student society known as the Apostles, to which Hallam read a number of papers that survive, including the essay "On Sympathy," extracted below. The son of the historian Henry Hallam, he was well-connected in literary and intellectual circles. He arranged for the publication of Tennyson's 1830 volume *Poems, Chiefly Lyrical*, originally planned by the two of them as a collaborative work, and reviewed it in an important essay, "On Some of the Characteristics of Modern Poetry, and on the Lyrical Poems of Alfred Tennyson" (*Englishman's Magazine* 1: 616–28). His own poems appeared in a separate volume, also in 1830; he also wrote criticism on Italian literature, and when he died was at work on what would have been the first English translation of Dante's *La Vita Nuova*. After completing his BA in 1832, Hallam became engaged to Emily Tennyson and prepared for a legal career; he died of a ruptured cerebral aneurysm in 1833 while traveling with his father in Vienna. Some of his writings were gathered by his father and published in 1834 as *Remains in Verse and Prose of Arthur Henry Hallam*; this volume provides the text followed in the selections below, except for the sonnet to Emily Tennyson, which is reprinted from T.H. Vail Motter's *The Writings of Arthur Hallam* (Modern Language Association: New York, 1943).]

1. Meditative Fragment 1 (1829)

[This blank verse meditation was addressed to Hallam's friend J.M. Gaskell in 1829. The two were classmates at Eton and in 1828 had traveled together in Italy.]

My bosom-friend, 'tis long since we have look'd
Upon each other's face; and God may will
It shall be longer, ere we meet again.
Awhile it seem'd most strange unto my heart
That I should mourn, and thou not nigh to cheer;   5

That I should shrink 'mid perils, and thy spirit
Far away, far, powerless to brave them with me.
Now am I used to wear a lonesome heart
About me; now the agencies of ill
Have so oppressed my inward, absolute self,   10
That feelings shared, and fully answered, scarce
Would seem my own. Like a bright, singular dream
Is parted from me that strong sense of love,
Which, as one invisible glory, lay
On both our souls, and dwelt in us, so far   15
As we did dwell in it. A mighty presence!
Almighty, had our wills but been confirmed
In consciousness of their immortal strength,
Given by that inconceivable will eterne
For a pure birthright, when the blank of things   20
First owned a motive power that was not God.
But thou—thy brow has ta'en no brand of grief:
Thine eyes look cheerful, even as when we stood
By Arno,[1] talking of the maid we loved.
In sooth I envy thee; thou seemest pure: 25
But I am seared: He in whom lies the world
Is coiled round the fibres of my heart,
And with his serpentine, thought-withering gaze
Doth fascinate the sovran[2] rational eye.
There is another world: and some have deem'd   30
It is a world of music, and of light,
And human voices, and delightful forms,
Where the material shall no more be cursed
By dominance of evil, but become
A beauteous evolution of pure spirit,   35
Opposite, but not warring, rather yielding
New grace, and evidence of liberty.
Oh, may we recognize each other there,
My bosom friend! May we cleave to each other
And love once more together! Pray for me,   40
That such may be the glory of our end.

---

1 The Italian river Arno runs through Florence.
2 An alternate spelling of sovereign.

2. Sonnet [After first meeting Emily Tennyson] (1829)

How is't for every glance of thine I find
A thousand recognitions seem to float
Up from my heart, and thro' my darkened mind,
Taking me with the sweetness of old thought?
I ne'er had seen thee: never was my sight   5
Made holy by a vision like to thee.
Whence is this riddle then? Art thou not She
Who in my Sais-temple[1] was a light
Behind all veils of thought, and fantasy,
A dim, yet beautiful Idea of one   10
Perfect in womanhood, in Love alone,
Making the earth golden with hope and joy?
And now thou com'st embodied to destroy
My grief with earnest eyes and music tone.

3. Sonnet [The garden trees] (1831)

The garden trees are busy with the shower
That fell ere sunset; now methinks they talk,
Lowly and sweetly as befits the hour,
One to another down the grassy walk.
Hark the laburnum from his opening flower   5
This cherry-creeper greets in whisper light,
While the grim fir, rejoicing in the night,
Hoarse mutters to the murmuring sycamore.
What shall I deem their converse? would they hail
The wild grey light that fronts yon massive cloud,   10
Or the half bow, rising like pillared fire?
Or are they sighing faintly for desire
That with May dawn their leaves may be o'erflowed,
And dews about their feet may never fail?

4. From "On Sympathy" (1830)

[Hallam read this essay to the Apostles in 1830; it combines a point of departure in associationist psychology, which has its roots in British empirical philosophy, with an idealist understanding of the "pre-established harmony in mind." The strongest literary influence on the essay

---

1 A reference to Plutarch's description of the temple at Sais, Egypt. See note 2 to *In Memoriam* section 56, p. 81.

is Wordsworth's; see especially the discussion in the "Preface to the *Lyrical Ballads*" (1802) of the poet as "pleased with his own passions" and "delighting to contemplate similar passions."]

Is it necessary to consider sympathy as an ultimate principle, or are there grounds for supposing it to be generated by association out of primary pleasures and pains?

It was my first intention to have given you an Essay on a much more copious subject. I wished to detail the successive formations of the virtuous affections from simple feelings of sympathy, and to examine the true nature of the moral sentiments. This is much more interesting to my mind than the actual subject of the following Essay, but I began with it, and I had not time to get beyond it. The admission of sympathy as an ultimate principle would not invalidate any subsequent conclusions respecting the virtues that arise out of it, but the contrary opinion will perhaps give so clear an impression of the great powers of association, as to help very considerably the future investigation. And in itself I think the question a very curious and pleasing one. Before I begin to discuss it, I must premise that the word sympathy, which like most others in moral science has a fluctuating import, is used in this Essay to denote the simple affection of the soul, by which it is pleased with another's pleasure and pained with another's pain, immediately and for their own sakes.

Let us take the soul at that precise moment in which she becomes assured that another soul exists. From tones, gestures, and other objects of sensation she has inferred that existence according to the simplest rules of association. Some philosophers, indeed, conceive an original instinct by which we infer design, and therefore mental existence, from the phenomena of animal motion, and the expressions of voice and countenance. I have no fondness, I confess, for these easy limitations of inquiry, these instincts, so fashionable in certain schools, and I know not why any new principle should be invented to account for one of these plainest of all associative processes. Be this as it may, the soul, then, has become aware of another individual subject, capable of thoughts and feelings like her own. How does this discovery affect her? It is possible she may feel pleasure in the mere knowledge of mere existence in this other subject; since it is probable that pleasure is inherent in the exercise of all the soul's capacities as such, and, therefore, the idea of a new similar set of capacities may irresistibly call up the idea, and the reality of pleasure. For association, I need hardly observe, does not only produce ideas of what in the past is similar to the present, but revives in many cases the feelings themselves. But as these probabilities are rather of a shadowy complexion, let us move a step further. The person thus recognised by the soul will probably have been occupied in acts of kindness towards it, by which indeed its attention was first attracted and the recognition rendered possible. Before that recognition, therefore, pleasure has been associated with that person, as a mere object. The infant cannot separate the sensations of nourishment from the form of his nurse or mother. But the expressions of voice and countenance in the person conferring this or any other pleasure were themselves agreeable, and such as indicate internal pleasure in that person. So soon, therefore, as the infant makes the recognition we spoke of, that is, assumes a conscious subject of those expressions, he is competent to make a second assumption, to wit, that the looks and tones in the other being, which accompany his own pleasure, are accompanied at the same time by pleasure in that other. Hence, wherever he perceives the indications of another's joy, he is prepared to rejoice, and, by parity of reasoning, wherever he perceives indications of pain, he is grieved; because those painful appearances have been connected by him with the absence of pleasurable sensations to himself, or even the positive presence of painful ones. A great step is thus gained in the soul's progress. She is immediately pleased by another's pleasure, and pained by another's pain. Close upon the experience of pleasure follows desire. As the soul in its first developement, within the sphere of itself, desired the recurrence of that object which had gratified it, so now, having connected its pleasure with that of another, she connects her desire with his desire. So also from the correspondence of pains will arise a correspondence of *aversions*, by which I mean *active dislikes*, the opposites of desire. Thus the machinery of sympathy, it might seem, would be complete; and since I have exhibited a legitimate process, by which the soul might arrive at a state precisely answering to the definition with which I set out, you may expect perhaps that the argument of this Essay is already terminated. Indeed some philosophers appear to consider this a complete account of the matter. But when I reflect on the peculiar force of sympathy itself, and the equivalent strength of those reflex sentiments regarding it, which I shall come presently to examine, I cannot but think something more is wanted. It seems to me that several processes of association operate simultaneously in the same direction, and that the united power of all imparts a character to this portion of our nature which each taken singly would not be able to produce. Let us again consider the soul at the starting-point, where it recognises a kindred being. The discovery is made, and the soul dwells upon it fondly, wishing to justify its own inference, and anxiously seeking for means of verification. Every new expression of feeling in the other being, the object of its contemplation, becomes an additional evidence. The more it can discern of pleasure, the more it becomes confirmed in its belief. I have alluded to the probability that every new exercise of a new function, every change of state, is to the soul an enjoyment. Pain may supervene, but in the nature of the thing, to feel, to live, is to enjoy. Pleasure, therefore, will be the surest sign of life to the soul. Hence there is the strongest possible inducement to be pleased with those marks of pleasure in another, which justify, as it were, the assumed similarity of that other to its own nature. Marks of pain, in a less degree, will also be proofs. How then, I may be asked, does it happen we are not pleased with the pain of our fellow-being? Because another result of association here intervenes. The sudden interruption of any train of feeling in which the mind acquiesces, has a uniform tendency to displease and shock us. When the perception of suffering in another interferes with our satisfaction in contemplating him, and in pursuing our process of verification, if I may so call it, this contrast produces pain. Besides, as the image of his enjoyment recalled images, and thereby awoke realities of pleasure in ourselves, so the perception of suffering makes us recollect our own suffering, and causes us to suffer. Thus by a second chain of associated feelings, the soul arrives at the same result, at union of joys and sorrows, in other words, at sympathy. I should remark, however, that compassion is not unmixed pain, and the pleasure mingling with it may still be legitimately referred to that assurance of life, which the marks of suffering afford. I shall now proceed to a third principle, from which the same result may be deduced. This is the principle of imitation. All animals are imitative. To repeat desires, volitions, actions, is the unquestionable tendency of conscious beings. It was a profound remark of Bishop Butler,[1] one of those anticipations of philosophic minds which are pregnant with theories, that perhaps the same simple power in the mind which disposes our actions to habitual courses, may be sufficient to account for the phenomena of memory. This is a very deep subject; and when we remember that the sphere of imitation is not confined to human, or even animal exertions, but appears to be co-extensive with organic life, we have reason to be cautious in dealing with this principle. So far, however, as it applies to our desires, there seems ground for supposing that the soul may desire another's gratification from the same impulse that leads a monkey to mimic the gestures of a man. Novelty is in itself an evident source of pleasure. To become something new, to add a mode of being to those we have experienced, is a temptation alike to the lisping infant in the cradle and old man on the verge of the grave. This may partly arise from that essential inherence of

---

1 Bishop Joseph Butler (1692–1752), author of *Analogy of Religion, Natural and Revealed* (1736).

pleasure in every state to which I have alluded, partly from a pleasure of contrast and surprise felt by the soul on gaining a new position. Now nothing can be more new than such a foreign capacity of enjoyment as the soul has here discovered. To become this new thing, to imitate, in a word, the discovered agent, no less in the internal than the outward elements of action, will naturally be the endeavour of faculties already accustomed in their own developement to numberless courses of imitation. For we imitate our previous acts in order to establish our very earliest knowledge. Through the medium of imitation alone, automatic notions become voluntary. It is then possible that through the desire to feel as another feels, we may come to feel so.

I know not whether I have succeeded in stating with tolerable clearness these three processes by which I conceive the association principle to operate in the production of sympathy. The number, however, is not yet exhausted, and those that remain to be described are perhaps more important, and will carry us more to the bottom of the matter, although for this very reason it will be difficult to avoid some obscurity in speaking of them. Some of you, perhaps, may be disposed to set me down as a mystic, for what I am about to say; just as some of you may have despised me as a mechanist, or a materialist, on account of what I have said already. In one and the other, however, I proceed upon tangible facts, or upon probabilities directly issuing out of such facts. It is an ultimate fact of consciousness, that the soul exists as one subject in various successive states. Our belief in this is the foundation of all reasoning. Far back as memory can carry us, or far forward as anticipation can travel unrestrained, the remembered state in the one case, the imagined one in the other, are forms of self. With the first dawn of feeling began the conception of existence, distinct from that of the moment in which the conception arose: hope, desire, apprehension, aversion, soon made the soul live entirely in reference to things non-existent. But what were these things? Possible conditions of the soul, the same undivided soul which existed in the conception and desire of them. Wide, therefore, as that universe might be, which comprehended for the imagination all varieties of untried consciousness, it was no wider than that self which imagined it. Material objects were indeed perceived as external. But how? As unknown limits of the soul's activity, they were not a part of subjective consciousness, they defined, restrained, and regulated it. Still the soul attributed itself to every consciousness, past or future. At length the discovery of another being is made. Another being, another subject, conscious, having a world of feelings like the soul's own world! How, how can the soul imagine feeling which is not its own? I repeat, she realizes this conception only by considering the other being as a separate part of self, a state of her own consciousness existing apart from the present, just as imagined states exist in the future. Thus absorbing, if I may speak so, this other being into her universal nature, the soul transfers at once her own feelings and adopts those of the new-comer. It is very possible there may be nothing in this notion of mine, which I doubt not many of you will think too refined. But it seems to deserve attentive consideration. The force of it lies in a supposed difficulty attending the structure of our consciousness; a difficulty of conceiving any existence, except in the way of matter, external to the conceiving mind. It may be objected, however, that this conjectural explanation is after all no explanation, since it can only account for an interest taken in the other being, but not for a coalition of pleasures or pains. The supposed identification is not assuredly closer than that which exists between the past and the present in ourselves, yet how often does our actual self desire different objects from those which allured us in a previous condition! The objection is weighty, but let us see what may be said against it. The soul, we have seen, exists as one permanent subject of innumerable successive states. But not only is there unity of subject, there is likewise a tendency to unity of form. The order of nature is uniform under the sway of invariable laws, the same phenomena perpetually recur. And there is a pre-established harmony in mind by which it anticipates this uniformity. I do not imagine any original principle distinct from association is necessary to account for this fact. But a fact it is, and the foundation of all inductive judgments. The soul naturally takes a great pleasure in this expectation of sameness, so perpetually answered, and affording scope for the developement of all faculties, and all dominion over surrounding things. Thus a wish for complete uniformity will arise wherever a similarity of any kind is observed. But a still deeper feeling is caused by that immediate knowledge of the past which is supplied by memory. To know a thing as past, and to know it as similar to something present, is a source of mingled emotions. There is pleasure, in so far as it is a revelation of self; but there is pain, in so far that it is a divided self, a being at once our own and not our own, a portion cut away from what we feel, nevertheless, to be single and indivisible. I fear these expressions will be thought to border on mysticism. Yet I must believe that if any one, in the least accustomed to analyze his feelings, will take the pains to reflect on it, he may remember moments in which the burden of this mystery[1] has lain heavy on him; in which he has felt it miserable to exist, as it were, piecemeal, and in the continual flux of a stream; in which he has wondered, as at a new thing, how we can be, and have been, and not be

---

1 Compare Wordsworth, "Lines Written a Few Miles Above Tintern Abbey" 38: "the burthen of the mystery."

that which we have been. But the yearnings of the human soul for the irrecoverable past are checked by a stern knowledge of impossibility. So also in its eager rushings towards the future, its desire of that mysterious something which now is not, but which in another minute we shall be, the soul is checked by a lesson of experience, which teaches her that she cannot carry into that future the actual mode of her existence. But were these impossibilities removed, were it conceivable that the soul in one state should coexist with the soul in another, how impetuous would be that desire of reunion, which even the awful laws of time cannot entirely forbid! The cause, you will say, is inconceivable. Not so; it is the very case before us. The soul, we have seen, contemplates a separate being as a separate state of itself, the only being it can conceive. But the two exist simultaneously. Therefore that impetuous desire arises. Therefore, in her anxiety to break down all obstacles, and to amalgamate two portions of her divided substance, she will hasten to blend emotions and desires with those apparent in the kindred spirit. I request it may be considered whether these two circumstances, to wit, the anticipation of uniformity natural to the soul, and the melancholy pleasure occasioned by the idea of time, are not sufficient to remove the objection stated above, and finally, whether this notion of the soul's identifying the perceived being with herself may not be thought to have some weight, especially when such identification is relied upon as a concurrent cause with the others first spoken of....

It was my intention to have continued this Essay so as to exhibit the rise and progress of those pains and pleasures, aversions and desires, which arise in the soul in consequence of sympathy, and whose peculiar force I should have shewn to depend on the peculiar powers of the several feelings composing sympathy. These may be comprised under the terms remorse and moral satisfaction, or any equivalent, there being no single word. I should then have detailed the gradual generation of the virtues from the primary feelings of sympathy, taking for my guide the principle of association. I should have shewn gratitude, resentment, justice, veracity, inevitably resulting from combinations of the primary pleasures and pains with their offspring, sympathy, and with those reflex sentiments which regard it. I should have shewn these sentiments overshadowing the generated affections as they had protected the parent one, and acquiring at every step additional force and authority. I should have attempted to prove that moral approbation and blame are not applied to agents and actions unconnected with ourselves in virtue of any faculty of approving or any *realist* ideas of Right and Wrong, but by a simple extension of sympathy, strengthened as that passion has become by the reaction of all the secondary affections, according to the obvious nature of association. I should have spoken of the self-regarding virtues, temperance, fortitude, prudence, and explained how far they come under the jurisdiction of the reflex sentiments. Finally, I should have endeavored to express how sympathy receives its final consummation, and the moral sentiments their strongest sanction, from the aid of religion, the power which binds over again (religare, according to some, is the etymology of the word) what the bond of nature was unable adequately to secure. But these considerations I must leave to some other and more favourable opportunity.

Appendix B: Writings on Natural History, Taxonomy, and Evolution, 1802–44

1. From William Paley, *Natural Theology; or, Evidences of the Existence and Attributes of the Deity* (1802)

[William Paley (1743–1805) was a British philosopher of science and Christian apologist. As a tutor at Christ's College, Cambridge, Paley published *The Principles of Moral and Political Philosophy* (1785), which subsequently became required reading as part of the university's examinations. In 1794 Paley published *View of the Evidences of Christianity*, his second contribution to the field of Christian apologetics, which was also made required reading at Cambridge. While *The Principles* and *Evidences* helped to build Paley's reputation as a political and moral philosopher and a defender of the faith, it was his final publication, *Natural Theology; or, Evidences of the Existence and Attributes of the Deity* (1802), that won him lasting renown. In *Natural Theology*, Paley infers the existence of God by finding evidence of God's design in the order and beauty of the social and material world. Abounding in metaphor, *Natural Theology* demonstrates Paley as a master of rhetoric, as he cumulatively builds his argument through a string of analogies, most famously that of God as watchmaker. The text of this selection is from the 1825 *Complete Works of William Paley D.D.*]

From Chapter 1

In crossing a heath, suppose I pitched my foot against a *stone*, and were asked how the stone came to be there: I might possibly answer, that for any thing I knew to the contrary, it had lain there for ever: nor would it perhaps be very easy to shew the absurdity of this answer. But suppose I had found a *watch* upon the ground, and it should be inquired how the watch happened to be in that place; I should hardly think of the answer which I had before given, that, for any thing I knew, the watch might have always been there. Yet why should not this answer serve for the watch as well as for the stone? why is it not as admissible in the second case, as in the first? For this reason, and for no other, viz. that, when we come to inspect the watch, we perceive (what we could not discover in the stone) that its several parts are framed and put together for a purpose, *e.g.* that they are so formed and adjusted as to produce motion, and that motion so regulated as to point out the hour of the day.... This mechanism being observed ... the inference, we think, is inevitable, that the watch must have had a maker; that there must have existed, at some time, and at some place or other, an artificer or artificers, who formed it for the purpose which we find it actually to answer; who comprehended its construction, and designed its use.

From Chapter 2

Suppose, in the next place, that the person who found the watch, should, after some time, discover that, in addition to all the properties which he had hitherto observed in it, it possessed the unexpected property of producing, in the course of its movement, another watch like itself (the thing is inconceivable); that it contained within it a mechanism, a system of parts, a mould for instance, or a complex adjustment of lathes, files, and other tools, evidently and separately calculated for this purpose; let us inquire, what effect ought such a discovery to have upon his former conclusion....

The conclusion which the *first* examination of the watch, of its works, construction, and movement, suggested, was, that it must have had, for the cause and author of that construction, an artificer, who understood its mechanism, and designed its use. This conclusion is invincible. A *second* examination presents us with a new discovery. The watch is found, in the course of its movement, to produce another watch, similar to itself; and not only so, but we perceive in it a system or organization, separately calculated for that purpose. What effect would this discovery have, or ought it to have, upon our former inference? What ... but to increase, beyond measure, our admiration of the skill which had been employed in the formation of such a machine? Or shall it, instead of this, all at once turn us round to an opposite conclusion, viz. that no art or skill whatever has been concerned in the business, although all other evidences of art and skill remain as they were, and this last and supreme piece of art be now added to the rest? Can this be maintained without absurdity? Yet this is atheism.

From Chapter 3

This is atheism: for every indication of contrivance, every manifestation of design, which existed in the watch, exists in the works of nature; with the difference, on the side of nature, of being greater and more, and that in a degree which exceeds all computation. I mean, that the contrivances of nature surpass the contrivances of art, in the complexity, subtilty, and curiosity, of the mechanism; and still more, if possible, do they go beyond them in number and variety; yet, in a multitude of cases, are not less evidently contrivances, not less evidently accommodated to their end, or suited to their office, than are the most perfect productions of human ingenuity.

I know no better method of introducing so large a subject, than that of comparing a single thing with a single thing; an eye, for example, with a telescope. As far as the examination of the instrument goes, there is precisely the same proof that the eye was made for vision, as there is that the telescope was made for assisting it. They are made upon the same principles; both being adjusted to the laws by which the transmission and refraction of rays of light are regulated. I speak not of the origin of the laws themselves; but such laws being fixed, the construction, in both cases, is adapted for them. For instance; these laws require, in order to produce the same effect, that the rays of light, in passing from water into the eye, should be refracted by a more convex surface, than when it passes out of air into the eye. Accordingly we find that the eye of a fish, in that part of it called the crystalline lens, is much rounder than the eye of terrestrial animals. What plainer manifestation of design can there be than this difference? What could a mathematical instrument maker have done more, to shew his knowledge of his principle, his application of that knowledge, his suiting of his means to his end; I will not say to display the compass or excellence of his skill and art, for in these all comparison is indecorous, but to testify counsel, choice, consideration, purpose? ...

Observe a new-born child first lifting up its eyelids. What does the opening of the curtain discover? The anterior part of two pellucid globes, which, when they come to be examined, are found to be constructed upon strict optical principles; the self-same principles upon which we ourselves construct optical instruments. We find them perfect for the purpose of forming an image by refraction; composed of parts executing different offices: one part having fulfilled its office upon the pencil of light, delivering it over to the action of another part; that to a third, and so onward; the progressive action depending for its success upon the nicest and minutest adjustment of the parts concerned; yet these parts so in fact adjusted, as to produce, not by a simple action or effect, but by a combination of actions and effects, the result which is ultimately wanted. And forasmuch as this organ would have to operate under different circumstances, with strong degrees of light, and with weak degrees, upon near objects, and upon remote ones; and these differences demanded, according to the laws by which the transmission of light is regulated, a corresponding diversity of structure; that the aperture, for example, through which the light passes, should be larger or less; the lenses rounder or flatter, or that their distance from the tablet, upon which the picture is delineated, should be shortened or lengthened: this, I say, being the case, and the difficulty to which the eye was to be adapted, we find its several parts capable of being occasionally changed, and a most artificial apparatus provided to produce that change. This is far beyond the common regulator of a watch, which requires the touch of a foreign hand to set it....

But this, though much, is not the whole: by different species of animals the faculty we are describing is possessed, in degrees suited to the different range of vision which their mode of life, and of procuring their food, requires. *Birds*, for instance, in general, procure their food by means of their beak; and, the distance between the eye and the point of the beak being small, it becomes necessary that they should have the power of seeing very near objects distinctly. On the other hand, from being often elevated much above the ground, living in the air, and moving through it with great velocity, they require, for their safety, as well as for assisting them in descrying their prey, a power of seeing at a great distance; a power of which, in birds of rapine, surprising examples are given.

2. From Charles Lyell, *The Principles of Geology*, Vol. 1 (1830)

[Sir Charles Lyell (1797–1875) was a British lawyer who came to be the foremost geologist of his time. Lyell's great work *The Principles of Geology*, which saw twelve editions between 1830 and 1875, popularized a doctrine, first advanced by James Hutton, of the uniformity of geological processes in past and present ages. Lyell's uniformitarianism combines actualism—the principle that the geological processes that shaped the world as we know it are the same processes active today—with gradualism—the principle that geological change occurs incrementally, for example, through the infinitesimally slow process of the upheaval and subsidence of strata—and argues that the natural world is governed by fixed natural laws. With his incrementalist view of geological change, Lyell paved the way for Charles Darwin's theory of the origin of species by natural selection, though he was himself reluctant to accept the transmutation of species, and in the first nine editions of the *Principles* held that species are created in succession and thereafter continue without change. Tennyson read Lyell's *Principles* in 1837; the text of this selection is from the first edition.]

From Chapters 4–5

Hutton laboured to give fixed principles to geology, as Newton had succeeded in doing to astronomy; but in the former science too little progress had been made towards furnishing the necessary data to enable any philosopher, however great his genius, to realize so noble a project....

"The ruins of an older world," said Hutton, "are visible in the present structure of our planet, and the strata which now compose our continents have been once beneath the sea, and were formed out of the waste of pre-existing continents. The same forces are still destroying, by chemical decomposition or mechanical violence, even the hardest rocks, and transporting the materials to the sea, where they are spread out, and form strata analogous to those of more ancient date.... In the economy of the world," said [Hutton], "I can find no traces of a beginning, no prospect of an end;" and the declaration was the more startling when coupled with the doctrine, that all past changes on the globe had been brought about by the slow agency of existing causes. The imagination was first fatigued and overpowered by endeavouring to conceive the immensity of time required for the annihilation of whole continents by so insensible a process. Yet when the thoughts had wandered through these interminable periods, no resting place was assigned in the remotest distance. The oldest rocks were represented to be of a derivative nature, the last of an antecedent series, and that perhaps one of many pre-existing worlds. Such views of the immensity of past time, like those unfolded by the Newtonian philosophy in regard to space, were too vast to awaken ideas of sublimity unmixed with a painful sense of our incapacity to conceive a plan of such infinite extent.

From Chapter 9

It is, therefore, clear, that there is no foundation in geological facts, for the popular theory of the successive development of the animal and vegetable world, from the simplest to the most perfect forms;[1] and we shall now proceed to consider another question, whether the recent origin of man lends any support to the same doctrine, or how far the influence of man may be considered as such a deviation from the analogy of the order of things previously established, as to weaken our confidence in the uniformity of the course of nature....

In reasoning on the state of the globe immediately before our species was called into existence, we may assume that all the present causes were in operation, with the exception of man, until some geological arguments can be adduced to the contrary. We must be guided by the same rules of induction as when we speculate on the state of

---

1 Lyell here rejects the theory of the progressive transmutation and evolution of species advanced by Jean-Baptiste Lamarck in his *Philosophie Zoologique* (1809).

America in the interval that elapsed between the period of the introduction of man into Asia, the cradle of our race, and that of the arrival of the first adventurers on the shores of the New World. In that interval, we imagine the state of things to have gone on according to the order now observed in regions unoccupied by man. Even now, the waters of lakes, seas, and the great ocean, which teem with life, may be said to have no immediate relation to the human race—to be portions of the terrestrial system of which man has never taken, nor ever can take, possession, so that the greater part of the inhabited surface of the planet remains still as insensible to our presence, as before any isle or continent was appointed to be our residence.

The variations in the external configuration of the earth, and the successive changes in the races of animals and plants inhabiting the land and sea, which the geologist beholds when he restores in imagination the scenes presented by certain regions at former periods, are not more full of wonderful or inexplicable phenomena, than are those which a traveller would witness who traversed the globe from pole to pole. Or if there be more to astonish and perplex us in searching the records of the past, it is because one district may, in an indefinite lapse of ages, become the theatre of a greater number of extraordinary events, than the whole face of the globe can exhibit at one time. However great the multiplicity of new appearances, and however unexpected the aspect of things in different parts of the present surface, the observer would never imagine that he was transported from one system of things to another, because there would always be too many points of resemblance, and too much connexion between the characteristic features of each country visited in succession, to permit any doubt to arise as to the continuity and identity of the whole plan.

"In our globe," says Paley, "new countries are continually discovered, but the old laws of nature are always found in them: new plants perhaps, or animals, but always in company with plants and animals which we already know, and always possessing many of the same general properties. We never get amongst such original, or totally different modes of existence, as to indicate that we are come into the province of a different Creator, or under the direction of a different will. In truth, the same order of things attends us wherever we go."[1] But the geologist is in danger of drawing a contrary inference, because he has the power of passing rapidly from the events of one period to those of another—of beholding, at one glance, the effects of causes which may have happened at intervals of time incalculably remote, and during which, nevertheless, no local circumstances may have

---

1 *Natural Theology*, Chap. xxv. [Lyell's note]

occurred to mark that there is a great chasm in the chronological series of nature's archives. In the vast interval of time which may really have elapsed between the results of operations thus compared, the physical condition of the earth may, by slow and insensible modifications, have become entirely altered, one or more races of organic beings may have passed away, and yet have left behind, in the particular region under contemplation, no trace of their existence. To a mind unconscious of these intermediate links in the chain of events, the passage from one state of things to another must appear so violent, that the idea of revolutions in the system inevitably suggests itself....

But if, instead of inverting the natural order of inquiry, we cautiously proceed in our investigations, from the known to the unknown, and begin by studying the most modern periods of the earth's history, attempting afterwards to decipher the monuments of more ancient changes, we can never so far lose sight of analogy, as to suspect that we have arrived at a new system, governed by different physical laws. In more recent formations, consisting often of strata of great thickness, the shells of the present seas and lakes, and the remains of animals and plants now living on the land, are imbedded in great numbers. In those of more ancient date, many of the same species are found associated with others now extinct. These unknown kinds again are observed in strata of still higher antiquity, connected with a great number of others which have also no living representatives, till at length we arrive at periods of which the monuments contain exclusively the remains of species with many genera foreign to the present creation. But even in the oldest rocks which contain organic remains, some genera of marine animals are recognized, of which species still exist in our seas, and these are repeated at different intervals in all the intermediate groups of strata, attesting that, amidst the great variety of revolutions of which the earth's surface has been the theatre, there has never been a departure from the conditions necessary for the existence of certain unaltered types of organization....

The geologist who yields implicit assent to the truth of these principles, will deem it incumbent on him to examine with minute attention all the changes now in progress on the earth, and will regard every fact collected respecting the causes in diurnal action, as affording him a key to the interpretation of some mystery in the archives of remote ages. Our estimate, indeed, of the value of all geological evidence, and the interest derived from the investigation of the earth's history, must depend entirely on the degree of confidence which we feel in regard to the permanency of the laws of nature. Their immutable constancy alone can enable us to reason from analogy, by the strict rules of induction, respecting the events of former ages, or, by a comparison of the state of things at two distinct geological epochs, to arrive at the knowledge of general principles in the economy of our terrestrial system.

The uniformity of the plan being once assumed, events which have occurred at the most distant periods in the animate and inanimate world will be acknowledged to throw light on each other, and the deficiency of our information respecting some of the most obscure parts of the present creation will be removed. For as by studying the external configuration of the existing land and its inhabitants, we may restore in imagination the appearance of the ancient continents which have passed away, so may we obtain from the deposits of ancient seas and lakes an insight into the nature of the subaqueous processes now in operation, and of many forms of organic life, which, though now existing, are veiled from our sight. Rocks, also produced by subterranean fire in former ages at great depths in the bowels of the earth, present us, when upraised by gradual movements, and exposed to the light of heaven, with an image of those changes which the deep-seated volcano may now occasion in the nether regions. Thus, although we are mere sojourners on the surface of the planet, chained to a mere point in space, enduring but for a moment of time, the human mind is not only enabled to number worlds beyond the unassisted ken of mortal eye, but to trace the events of indefinite ages before the creation of our race, and is not even withheld from penetrating into the dark secrets of the ocean, or the interior of the solid globe; free, like the spirit which the poet described as animating the universe,

———ire per omnes
Terrasque tractusque maris, coelumque profundum.[1]

From Chapter 14

We may now conclude our remarks on deltas, observing that, imperfect as is our information of the changes which they have undergone within the last three thousand years, they are sufficient to show how constant an interchange of sea and land is taking place on the face of our globe. In the Mediterranean alone, many flourishing inland towns, and a still greater number of ports, now stand where the sea rolled its waves since the era when civilized nations first grew up in Europe. If we could compare with equal accuracy the ancient and actual state of all the islands and continents, we should probably discover that millions of our race are now supported by lands situated where deep seas prevailed in earlier ages. In many districts not yet

---

1 Lyell quotes Virgil, *Georgics* 4.221–22, where God "pervades all things, earth and sea's expanse and heaven's depth."

occupied by man, land animals and forests now abound where the anchor once sank into the oozy bottom. We shall find, on inquiry, that inroads of the ocean have been no less considerable; and when to these revolutions produced by aqueous causes, we add analogous changes wrought by igneous agency, we shall, perhaps, acknowledge the justice of the conclusion of a great philosopher of antiquity, when he declared that the whole land and sea on our globe periodically changed places.[1]

3. From Robert Chambers, *Vestiges of the Natural History of Creation* (1844)

[Robert Chambers (1802–71) was a Scottish author, publisher, geologist, phrenologist, and evolutionist, best remembered for his treatise on the progressive transmutation of species and the development of the cosmos, published anonymously in 1844 as *Vestiges of the Natural History of Creation*. The book was an immediate best-seller and retained its popularity throughout the century, in spite of denunciations from both the scientific and religious establishments. While the work was anonymous when published and remained so until its twelfth edition in 1884, by the mid-1850s Chambers was generally credited with *Vestiges*'s authorship. On reading a review of the first edition, Tennyson had his publisher send him a copy, writing that "it seems to contain many speculations with which I have been familiar for years, and on which I have written more than one poem" (*Letters* 1: 230). The first edition text is followed in these selections.]

From Chapter 12

In pursuing the progress of the development of both plants and animals upon the globe, we have seen an advance in both cases, along the line leading to the higher forms of organization. Amongst plants, we have first sea-weeds, afterwards land plants; and amongst these the simpler (cellular and cryptogamic) before the more complex. In the department of zoology, we see zoophytes, radiata, mollusca, articulata, existing for ages before there were any higher forms. The first step forward gives fishes, the humblest class of the vertebrata; and, moreover, the earliest fishes partake of the character of the next lowest sub-kingdom, the articulata. Afterwards come land animals, of which the first are reptiles, universally allowed to be the type next in advance from fishes, and to be connected with these by the links of an insensible gradation. From reptiles we advance to birds, and thence to mam-

---

1 Aristotle, *Meteorology* 1.14.

malia which are commenced by marsupialia, acknowledgedly low forms in their class. That there is thus a progress of some kind, the most superficial glance at the geological history is sufficient to convince us. Indeed the doctrine of the gradation of animal forms has received a remarkable support from the discoveries of this science, as several types formerly wanting to a completion of the series have been found in a fossil state....

A candid consideration of all these circumstances can scarcely fail to introduce into our minds a somewhat different idea of organic creation from what has hitherto been generally entertained. That God created animated beings, as well as the terraqueous theatre of their being, is a fact so powerfully evidenced, and so universally received, that I at once take it for granted. But in the particulars of this so highly supported idea, we surely here see cause for some re-consideration. It may now be inquired,—In what way was the creation of animated beings effected? The ordinary notion may, I think, be not unjustly described as this,—that the Almighty author produced the progenitors of all existing species by some sort of personal or immediate exertion. But how does this notion comport with what we have seen of the gradual advance of species, from the humblest to the highest? How can we suppose an immediate exertion of this creative power at one time to produce zoophytes, another time to add a few marine mollusks, another to bring in one or two conchifers, again to produce crustaceous fishes, again perfect fishes, and so on to the end? This would surely be to take a very mean view of the Creative Power—to, in short, anthropomorphize it, or reduce it to some such character as that borne by the ordinary proceedings of mankind. And yet this would be unavoidable; for that the organic creation was thus progressive through a long space of time, rests on evidence which nothing can overturn or gainsay. Some other idea must then be come to with regard to *the mode* in which the Divine Author proceeded in the organic creation. Let us seek in the history of the earth's formation for a new suggestion on this point. We have seen powerful evidence, that the construction of this globe and its associates, and inferentially that of all the other globes of space, was the result, not of any immediate or personal exertion on the part of the Deity, but of natural laws which are expressions of his will. What is to hinder our supposing that the organic creation is also a result of natural laws, which are in like manner an expression of his will? More than this, the fact of the cosmical arrangements being an effect of natural law, is a powerful argument for the organic arrangements being so likewise, for how can we suppose that the august Being who brought all these countless worlds into form by the simple establishment of a natural principle flowing from his mind, was to interfere personally and specially on every occasion when a new shell-fish or reptile was to be ushered into existence on *one* of these worlds? Surely this idea is too ridiculous to be for a moment entertained.

From Chapter 14

We shall now see an instance of development operating within the production of what approaches to the character of variety of species. It is fully established that a human family, tribe, or nation, is liable, in the course of generations, to be either advanced from a mean form to a higher one, or degraded from a higher to a lower, by the influence of the physical conditions in which it lives. The coarse features, and other structural peculiarities of the negro race only continue while these people live amidst the circumstances usually associated with barbarism. In a more temperate clime, and higher social state, the face and figure become greatly refined. The few African nations which possess any civilization also exhibit forms approaching the European; and when the same people in the United States of America have enjoyed a within-door life for several generations, they assimilate to the whites amongst whom they live. On the other hand, there are authentic instances of a people originally well-formed and good-looking, being brought, by imperfect diet and a variety of physical hardships, to a meaner form. It is remarkable that prominence of the jaws, a recession and diminution of the cranium, and an elongation and attenuation of the limbs, are peculiarities always produced by these miserable conditions, for they indicate an unequivocal retrogression towards the type of the lower animals. Thus we see nature alike willing to go back and forward. Both effects are simply the result of the operation of the law of development in the generative system. Give good conditions, it advances; bad ones, it recedes. Now, perhaps, it is only because there is no longer a possibility, in the higher types of being, of giving sufficiently favourable conditions to carry on species to species, that we see the operation of the law so far limited.

From Chapter 15

Man, then, considered zoologically, and without regard to the distinct character assigned to him by theology, simply takes his place as the type of all types of the animal kingdom, the true and unmistakable head of animated nature upon this earth....

There is no other family approaching to this [that of the human race] in importance, which presents but one species.... It is startling to find such an appearance of imperfection in the circle to which man belongs, and the ideas which rise in consequence are not less startling.

Is our race but the initial of the grand crowning type? Are there yet to be species superior to us in organization, purer in feeling, more powerful in device and act, and who shall take a rule over us! There is in this nothing improbable on other grounds. The present race, rude and impulsive as it is, is perhaps the best adapted to the present state of things in the world; but the external world goes through slow and gradual changes, which may leave it in time a much serener field of existence. There may then be occasion for a nobler type of humanity, which shall complete the zoological circle on this planet, and realize some of the dreams of the purest spirits of the present race.

From Chapter 18

It is clear, moreover, from the whole scope of the natural laws, that the individual, as far as the present sphere of being is concerned, is to the Author of Nature a consideration of inferior moment. Everywhere we see the arrangements for the species perfect; the individual is left, as it were, to take his chance amidst the *melee* of the various laws affecting him. If he be found inferiorly endowed, or ill befalls him, there was at least no partiality against him. The system has the fairness of a lottery, in which every one has the like chance of drawing the prize....

It occurs to me ... that there is nothing to prevent our regarding God as revealed to us in two capacities; first, as the author and sustainer of nature by fixed laws, and second, as our spiritual father, ever present in all that we do and think, and to be yet more clearly revealed to us. It may be that we are left by him to all the contingencies arising in the course of the fixed procedure of mundane affairs, and yet are capable of communing with him, may be affected in the strain of our life by results flowing from that communion, and are in the end received into his presence. There may be, behind the screen of nature, a system of mercy and grace which is to make up for all casualties endured here, and the very largeness of which is what makes these casualties a matter of indifference to God. For the existence of such a system, the actual constitution of nature is indeed a powerful argument. The reasoning may proceed thus:—the system of nature assures us that benevolence is a leading principle in the Divine Mind. But that system is at the same time deficient in a means of making this benevolence of invariable operation. To reconcile this to the character of the Deity, it is necessary to suppose that the present system is but a part of a whole, a stage in a Great Progress, and that the Redress is in reserve.

Appendix C: Victorian Courtship and Marriage in Fiction

[Idealized representations of courtship and marriage were staples of Victorian prose fiction, even more than of poetry. Indeed, their treatment of the topic was one of the areas in which the two genres, which had hitherto developed largely along separate lines, began to influence one another.]

1. From Mary Russell Mitford, *Our Village: Sketches of Rural Character and Scenery* (1824)

[Mary Russell Mitford (1787–1855) published her first volume of poetry in 1810, with three more following in the succeeding three years. During her early adulthood, however, her father's extravagance led to his ruin, and from 1820, when the family moved to a laborer's cottage in the village of Three Mile Cross, Mitford's poetic ambitions yielded to the need to earn money as a professional writer and woman of letters. She wrote plays and performed editorial work, but achieved her greatest fame as the author of prose sketches of rural life. The first series of sketches in *Our Village* were published in the *Lady's Magazine* beginning in 1822; they were gathered in book form in 1824. Four further volumes of sketches followed by 1832. *Our Village* directly influenced Tennyson's poetic representations of rural English life and courtship in "The Miller's Daughter" (1832) and "The Brook" (1855).]

From "Hannah"

At sixteen Hannah Wilson was, beyond a doubt, the prettiest girl in the village, and the best. Her beauty was quite in a different style from the common country rosebud—far more choice and rare. Its chief characteristic was modesty. A light youthful figure, exquisitely graceful and rapid in all its movements; springy, elastic, and buoyant as a bird, and almost as shy; a fair innocent face, with downcast blue eyes, and smiles and blushes coming and going almost with her thoughts; a low soft voice, sweet even in its monosyllables; a dress remarkable for neatness and propriety, and borrowing from her delicate beauty an air of superiority not its own;—such was the outward woman of Hannah. Her mind was very like her person; modest, graceful, gentle, affectionate, grateful, and generous above all. The generosity of the poor is always a very real and fine thing: they give what they want; and Hannah was of all poor people the most generous. She loved to give; it was her pleasure, her luxury. Rosy-cheeked apples, plums with the bloom on them, nosegays of cloves and blossomed myrtle; these were offerings which Hannah delighted to bring to those whom she loved, or those who had shown her kindness; whilst to such of her neighbours as needed other attentions than fruit and flowers, she would give her time, her assistance, her skill; for Hannah inherited her mother's dexterity in feminine employments, with something of her father's versatile power. Besides being an excellent laundress, she was accomplished in all the arts of the needle, millinery, dress-making, and plain work; a capital cutter-out, an incomparable mender, and endowed with a gift of altering, which made old things better than new. She had no rival at a *rifacimento*,[1] as half the turned gowns on the common can witness. As a dairy-woman, and a rearer of pigs and poultry, she was equally successful: none of her ducks and turkeys ever died of neglect or carelessness, or, to use the phrase of the poultry-yard on such occasions, of "ill luck." Hannah's fowls never dreamed of sliding out of the world in such an ignoble way; they all lived to be killed, to make a noise at their deaths, as chickens should do. She was also a famous "scholar;" kept accounts, wrote bills, read letters, and answered them; was a trusty accomptant, and a safe confidante. There was no end to Hannah's usefulness or Hannah's kindness; and her prudence was equal to either. Except to be kind or useful, she never left her home; attended no fairs, or revels, or Mayings; went no where but to church; and seldom made a nearer approach to rustic revelry than by standing at her own garden-gate on a Sunday evening, with her little sister in hand, to look at the lads and lasses on the green. In short, our village beauty had fairly reached her twentieth year without a sweetheart, without the slightest suspicion of her having ever written a love-letter on her own account; when, all on a sudden, appearances changed. She was missing at the "accustomed gate;" and one had seen a young man go into Dame Wilson's; and another had descried a trim elastic figure walking, not unaccompanied, down a shady lane....

Since the new marriage act,[2] we, who belong to country magistrates, have gained a priority over the rest of the parish in matrimonial news. We (the privileged) see on a work-day the names which the sabbath announces to the generality. Many a blushing awkward pair hath our little lame clerk (a sorry Cupid!) ushered in between dark and light to stammer and hacker, to bow and curtsy, to sign or make a mark, as it pleases Heaven. One Saturday, at the usual hour, the

---

1   Remaking (Italian).

2   The Marriage Act of 1823 established rules governing the registration and witnessing of weddings.

limping clerk made his appearance; and, walking through our little hall, I saw a fine athletic young man, the very image of health and vigour, mental and bodily, holding the hand of a young woman, who, with her head half buried in a geranium in the window, was turning bashfully away, listening, and yet not seeming to listen, to his tender whispers. The shrinking grace of that bending figure was not to be mistaken. "Hannah!" and she went aside with me, and a rapid series of questions and answers conveyed the story of the courtship. "William was," said Hannah, "a journeyman hatter in B. He had walked over one Sunday evening to see the cricketing, and then he came again. Her mother liked him. Every body liked her William—and she had promised—she was going—was it wrong?"—"Oh no!—and where are you to live?"—"William has got a room in B. He works for Mr. Smith, the rich hatter in the market-place, and Mr. Smith speaks of him—oh, so well! But William will not tell me where our room is. I suppose in some narrow street or lane, which he is afraid I shall not like, as our common is so pleasant. He little thinks—any where"—She stopped suddenly; but her blush and her clasped hands finished the sentence, "any where with him!"—"And when is the happy day?"— "On Monday fortnight, Madam," said the bridegroom elect, advancing with the little clerk to summon Hannah to the parlour, "the earliest day possible." He drew her arm through his, and we parted.

The Monday fortnight was a glorious morning; one of those rare November days when the sky and the air are soft and bright as in April. "What a beautiful day for Hannah!" was the first exclamation of the breakfast-table. "Did she tell you where they should dine?"—"No, Ma'am; I forgot to ask."—"I can tell you," said the master of the house, with somewhat of good-humoured importance in his air, somewhat of the look of a man who, having kept a secret as long as it was necessary, is not sorry to get rid of the burthen. "I can tell you: in London."—"In London!"—"Yes. Your little favourite has been in high luck. She has married the only son of one of the best and richest men in B., Mr. Smith, the great hatter. It is quite a romance," continued he: "William Smith walked over one Sunday evening to see a match at cricket. He saw our pretty Hannah, and forgot to look at the cricketers. After having gazed his fill, he approached to address her, and the little damsel was off like a bird. William did not like her less for that, and thought of her the more. He came again and again; and at last contrived to tame his wild dove, and even to get the *entrée* of the cottage. Hearing Hannah talk, is not the way to fall out of love with her. So William, at last finding his case serious, laid the matter before his father, and requested his consent to the marriage. Mr. Smith was at first a little startled; but William is an only son, and an excellent son; and, after talking with me, and looking at Hannah, (I believe her sweet face was the more eloquent advocate of the two,) he relented; and having a spice of his son's romance, finding that he had not mentioned his situation in life, he made a point of its being kept secret till the wedding-day. We have managed the business of settlements; and William, having discovered that his fair bride has some curiosity to see London, (a curiosity, by the bye, which I suspect she owes to you or poor Lucy,) intends taking her thither for a fortnight. He will then bring her home to one of the best houses in B., a fine garden, fine furniture, fine clothes, fine servants, and more money than she will know what to do with. Really the surprise of Lord E.'s farmer's daughter, when, thinking she had married his steward, he brought her to Burleigh, and installed her as its mistress, could hardly have been greater. I hope the shock will not kill Hannah though, as is said to have been the case with that poor lady."[1]—"Oh no! Hannah loves her husband too well. Any where with him!"

And I was right. Hannah has survived the shock. She is returned to B., and I have been to call on her. I never saw any thing so delicate and bride-like as she looked in her white gown and her lace mob, in a room light and simple, and tasteful and elegant, with nothing fine except some beautiful green-house plants. Her reception was a charming mixture of sweetness and modesty, a little more respectful than usual, and far more shamefaced! Poor thing! her cheeks must have pained her! But this was the only difference. In every thing else she is still the same Hannah, and has lost none of her old habits of kindness and gratitude. She was making a handsome matronly cap, evidently for her mother, and spoke, even with tears, of her new father's goodness to her and to Susan. She would fetch the cake and wine herself, and would gather, in spite of all remonstrance, some of her choice flowers as a parting nosegay. She did, indeed, just hint at her troubles with visitors and servants,—how strange and sad it was! seemed distressed at ringing the bell, and visibly shrank from the sound of a double knock. But, in spite of these calamities, Hannah is a very happy woman. The double rap was her husband's; and the glow on her cheek, and the smile on her lips and eyes when he appeared, spoke more plainly than ever, "Any where with him!"

2. From Charles Dickens, *David Copperfield* (1850)

[Charles Dickens (1812–70) novelist, social critic, and editor, was the greatest literary phenomenon of mid-nineteenth-century England. Beginning with *The Pickwick Papers* (1837), his 14 novels achieved

---

1 See Tennyson's poem "The Lord of Burleigh" (1842), which tells the story alluded to here.

unprecedented sales and introduced characters and styles of senti-
mental and comic writing that became known throughout the English-
speaking world. The selection below is drawn from *David Copperfield*,
Dickens's most autobiographical novel. In the first person, David nar-
rates the events leading up to his wedding to Dora Spenlow and those
of the day itself. As Dora's accepted suitor, David is permitted unac-
companied visits with her in the house where she lives with her aunts
Lavinia and Clarissa. As with the wedding at the close of *In Memo-
riam*, there is a certain melancholy attendant on this one, since neither
David nor Dora has any immediate living relatives and the wedding
has only been made possible by the death of Dora's father, who would
have forbidden it.]

From Chapter 43

Yes! I am going to be married to Dora! Miss Lavinia and Miss Clarissa
have given their consent; and if ever canary-birds were in a flutter,
they are. Miss Lavinia, self-charged with the superintendence of my
darling's wardrobe, is constantly cutting out brown-paper cuirasses,
and differing in opinion from a highly respectable young man, with a
long bundle, and a yard measure under his arm. A dressmaker, always
stabbed in the breast with a needle and thread, boards and lodges in
the house; and seems to me, eating, drinking, or sleeping, never to take
her thimble off. They make a lay-figure of my dear. They are always
sending for her to come and try something on. We can't be happy
together for five minutes in the evening, but some intrusive female
knocks at the door, and says, "Oh, if you please, Miss Dora, would you
step up-stairs!"

Miss Clarissa and my aunt roam all over London, to find out arti-
cles of furniture for Dora and me to look at. It would be better for
them to buy the goods at once, without this ceremony of inspection;
for, when we go to see a kitchen fender and meat-screen, Dora sees a
Chinese house for Jip [her dog], with little bells on the top, and prefers
that. And it takes a long time to accustom Jip to his new residence,
after we have bought it; whenever he goes in or out, he makes all the
little bells ring, and is horribly frightened....

The realisation of my boyish day-dreams is at hand. I am going to
take out the licence.

It is a little document to do so much; and Traddles [David's boy-
hood friend] contemplates it, as it lies upon my desk, half in admira-
tion, half in awe. There are the names in the sweet old visionary con-
nexion, David Copperfield and Dora Spenlow; and there, in the
corner, is that Parental Institution, the Stamp Office, which is so
benignantly interested in the various transactions of human life,

looking down upon our Union; and there is the Archbishop of Canterbury invoking a blessing on us in print, and doing it as cheap as could possibly be expected.

Nevertheless, I am in a dream, a flustered, happy, hurried dream. I can't believe that it is going to be; and yet I can't believe but that every one I pass in the street, must have some kind of perception, that I am to be married the day after to-morrow. The Surrogate knows me, when I go down to be sworn; and disposes of me easily, as if there were a Masonic understanding between us. Traddles is not at all wanted, but is in attendance as my general backer.

"I hope the next time you come here, my dear fellow," I say to Traddles, "it will be on the same errand for yourself. And I hope it will be soon." ...

Next day, too, when we all go in a flock to see the house—our house—Dora's and mine—I am quite unable to regard myself as its master. I seem to be there, by permission of somebody else. I half expect the real master to come home presently, and say he is glad to see me. Such a beautiful little house as it is, with everything so bright and new; with the flowers on the carpets looking as if freshly gathered, and the green leaves on the paper as if they had just come out; with the spotless muslin curtains, and the blushing rose-coloured furniture, and Dora's garden hat with the blue ribbon—do I remember, now, how I loved her in such another hat when I first knew her!—already hanging on its little peg; the guitar-case quite at home on its heels in a corner; and everybody tumbling over Jip's pagoda, which is much too big for the establishment.

Another happy evening, quite as unreal as all the rest of it, and I steal into the usual room before going away. Dora is not there. I suppose they have not done trying on yet. Miss Lavinia peeps in, and tells me mysteriously that she will not be long. She is rather long, notwithstanding; but by-and-by I hear a rustling at the door, and some one taps.

I say, "Come in!" but some one taps again.

I go to the door, wondering who it is; there, I meet a pair of bright eyes, and a blushing face; they are Dora's eyes and face, and Miss Lavinia has dressed her in tomorrow's dress, bonnet and all, for me to see. I take my little wife to my heart; and Miss Lavinia gives a little scream because I tumble the bonnet, and Dora laughs and cries at once, because I am so pleased, and I believe it less than ever.

"Do you think it pretty, Doady?" says Dora.

Pretty! I should rather think I did.

"And are you sure you like me very much?" says Dora.

The topic is fraught with such danger to the bonnet, that Miss Lavinia gives another little scream, and begs me to understand that

Dora is only to be looked at, and on no account to be touched. So Dora stands in a delightful state of confusion for a minute or two, to be admired; and then takes off her bonnet—looking so natural without it!—and runs away with it in her hand; and comes dancing down again in her own familiar dress, and asks Jip if I have got a beautiful little wife, and whether he'll forgive her for being married, and kneels down to make him stand upon the Cookery Book, for the last time in her single life.

I go home, more incredulous than ever, to a lodging that I have hard by; and get up very early in the morning, to ride to the Highgate road and fetch my aunt.

I have never seen my aunt in such state. She is dressed in lavender-coloured silk, and has a white bonnet on, and is amazing. Janet has dressed her, and is there to look at me. Peggotty is ready to go to church, intending to behold the ceremony from the gallery. Mr. Dick, who is to give my darling to me at the altar, has had his hair curled. Traddles, whom I have taken up by appointment at the turnpike, presents a dazzling combination of cream colour and light blue; and both he and Mr. Dick have a general effect upon them of being all gloves.

No doubt I see this, because I know it is so; but I am astray, and seem to see nothing. Nor do I believe anything whatever. Still, as we drive along in an open carriage, this fairy marriage is real enough to fill me with a sort of wondering pity for the unfortunate people who have no part in it, but are sweeping out the shops, and going to their daily occupations....

The rest is all a more or less incoherent dream.

A dream of their coming in with Dora; of the pew-opener arranging us, like a drill-sergeant, before the altar rails; of my wondering, even then, why pew-openers must always be the most disagreeable females procurable, and whether there is any religious dread of a disastrous infection of good humour which renders it indispensable to set those vessels of vinegar upon the road to Heaven.

Of the clergymen and clerk appearing; of a few boatmen and some other people strolling in; of an ancient mariner behind me, strongly flavouring the church with rum; of the service beginning in a deep voice, and our all being very attentive.

Of Miss Lavinia, who acts as a semi-auxiliary bridesmaid being the first to cry, and of her doing homage (as I take it) to the memory of Pidger, in sobs; of Miss Clarissa applying a smelling-bottle; of Agnes taking care of Dora; of my aunt endeavouring to represent herself as a model of sternness, with tears rolling down her face; of little Dora trembling very much, and making her responses in faint whispers.

Of our kneeling down together, side by side; of Dora's trembling less and less, but always clasping Agnes by the hand; of the service being got through, quietly and gravely; of our all looking at each other in an April state of smiles and tears, when it is over; of my young wife being hysterical in the vestry, and crying for her poor papa, her dear papa.

Of her soon cheering up again, and our signing the register all round. Of my going into the gallery for Peggotty to bring *her* to sign it; of Peggotty's hugging me in a corner, and telling me she saw my own dear mother married; of its being over, and our going away.

Of my walking so proudly and lovingly down the aisle with my sweet wife upon my arm, through a mist of half-seen people, pulpits, monuments, pews, fonts, organs, and church-windows, in which there flutter faint airs of association with my childish church at home, so long ago.

Of their whispering, as we pass, what a youthful couple we are, and what a pretty little wife she is. Of our all being so merry and talkative in the carriage going back. Of Sophy telling us that when she saw Traddles (whom I had entrusted with the licence) asked for it, she almost fainted, having been convinced that he would contrive to lose it, or to have his pocket picked. Of Agnes laughing gaily; and of Dora being so fond of Agnes that she will not be separated from her, but still keeps her hand.

Of there being a breakfast, with abundance of things, pretty and substantial, to eat and drink, whereof I partake, as I should do in any other dream, without the least perception of their flavour; eating and drinking, as I may say, nothing but love and marriage, and no more believing in the viands than in anything else.

Of my making a speech in the same dreamy fashion, without having an idea of what I want to say, beyond such as may be comprehended in the full conviction that I haven't said it. Of our being very sociably and simply happy (always in a dream though); and of Jip's having wedding cake, and its not agreeing with him afterwards.

Of the pair of hired post-horses being ready, and of Dora's going away to change her dress. Of my aunt and Miss Clarissa remaining with us; and our walking in the garden; and my aunt, who has made quite a speech at breakfast touching Dora's aunts, being mightily amused with herself, but a little proud of it too.

Of Dora's being ready, and of Miss Lavinia's hovering about her, loth to lose the pretty toy that has given her so much pleasant occupation. Of Dora's making a long series of surprised discoveries that she has forgotten all sorts of little things; and of everybody's running everywhere to fetch them.

Of their all closing about Dora, when at last she begins to say good-bye, looking with their bright colours and ribbons, like a bed of flowers. Of my darling being almost smothered among the flowers, and coming out, laughing and crying both together, to my jealous arms.

Of my wanting to carry Jip (who is to go along with us), and Dora's saying No, that she must carry him, or else he'll think she don't like him any more, now she is married, and will break his heart. Of our going, arm in arm, and Dora stopping and looking back, and saying, "If I have ever been cross or ungrateful to anybody, don't remember it!" and bursting into tears.

Of her waving her little hand, and our going away once more. Of her once more stopping and looking back, and hurrying to Agnes, and giving Agnes, above all the others, her last kisses and farewells.

We drive away together, and I awake from the dream. I believe it at last. It is my dear, dear, little wife beside me, whom I love so well! "Are you happy now, you foolish boy?" says Dora, "and sure you don't repent?"

Appendix D: The Poetic Sequence, 1827–54

[The poetic sequence was the major formal innovation of Victorian poetry and among the period's most characteristic genres. It enabled poets to retain the intense immediacy of lyric while competing with the newly ascendant genre of the novel on the grounds of social realism and narrative amplitude. Among the genre's forebears were classical and Renaissance poems based on the calendar, such as the eclogue and georgic. Some sequence poems, such as Keble's *Christian Year*, also found inspiration in seventeenth-century devotional sequences—notably George Herbert's *The Temple*—and in the tradition of metrical translation of the Hebrew Psalms. The most important poetic influence on Victorian poetic sequences, though, was the revival of interest in Renaissance sequences of love sonnets, including those of Dante and Petrarch and above all that of Shakespeare.]

1. **From John Keble, *The Christian Year: Thoughts in Verse for the Sundays and Holidays Throughout the Year* (1827)**

[John Keble (1792–1866) was a clergyman in the Church of England, a poet, and a leader of the High Church Oxford movement. His poetic sequence *The Christian Year* was first published in 1827 and went on to over a hundred editions during his lifetime, becoming one of the nineteenth century's bestselling volumes of poetry. The sequence includes a poem for each Sunday of the year, and poems for the Church of England's major holy days and its occasional liturgies, such as the service for the burial of the dead. Each poem is a meditation on an Old Testament or Gospel text assigned to be read in church on its date, and the sequence served its readers as an unofficial manual of devotion. Especially for the bereaved, this role was partly taken over later in the century by *In Memoriam*. The text of these selections is from the 103rd edition, published in 1867.]

Fourth Sunday in Lent

Joseph made haste; for his bowels did yearn upon his brother; and he sought where to weep; and he entered into his chamber, and wept there.

Genesis 43.30

There stood no man with him, while Joseph made himself known
unto his brethren.

Genesis 45.1

When Nature tries her finest touch,
    Weaving her vernal wreath,
Mark ye, how close she veils her round,
Not to be trac'd by sight or sound,
    Nor soil'd by ruder breath?   5

Who ever saw the earliest rose
    First open her sweet breast?
Or, when the summer sun goes down,
The first soft star in evening's crown
    Light up her gleaming crest?   10

Fondly we seek the dawning bloom
    On features wan and fair,—
The gazing eye no change can trace,
But look away a little space,
    Then turn, and, lo! 'tis there.   15

But there's a sweeter flower than e'er
    Blush'd on the rosy spray—
A brighter star, a richer bloom
Than e'er did western heaven illume
    At close of summer day.   20

'Tis Love, the last best gift of Heaven;
    Love, gentle, holy, pure;
But tenderer than a dove's soft eye,
The searching sun, the open sky,
    She never could endure.   25

E'en human Love will shrink from sight
    Here in the coarse rude earth:
How then should rash intruding glance
Break in upon *her* sacred trance
    Who boasts a heavenly birth?   30

So still and secret is her growth,
    Ever the truest heart,

Where deepest strikes her kindly root
For hope or joy, for flower or fruit,
     Least knows its happy part.   35

God only, and good angels, look
     Behind the blissful screen—
As when, triumphant o'er His woes,
The Son of God by moonlight rose,
     By all but Heaven unseen: 40

As when the holy Maid beheld
     Her risen Son and Lord:
Thought has not colours half so fair
That she to paint that hour may dare,
     In silence best ador'd.   45

The gracious Dove, that brought from Heaven
     The earnest of our bliss,
Of many a chosen witness telling,
On many a happy vision dwelling,
     Sings not a note of this.   50

So, truest image of the Christ,
     Old Israel's long-lost son,
What time, with sweet forgiving cheer,
He call'd his conscious brethren near,
     Would weep with them alone.   55

He could not trust his melting soul
     But in his Maker's sight—
Then why should gentle hearts and true
Bare to the rude world's withering view
     Their treasure of delight!   60

No—let the dainty rose awhile
     Her bashful fragrance hide—
Rend not her silken veil too soon,
But leave her, in her own soft noon,
     To flourish and abide.   65

Burial of the Dead

And when the Lord saw her, He had compassion on her, and said
unto her, Weep not. And He came and touched the bier; and they
that bare him stood still. And He said Young man, I say unto thee,
Arise.

Luke 7.13–14

Who says, the wan autumnal sun
      Beams with too faint a smile
To light up nature's face again,
And, though the year be on the wane,
      With thoughts of spring the heart beguile?   5

Waft him, thou soft September breeze,
      And gently lay him down
Within some circling woodland wall,
Where bright leaves, reddening ere they fall,
      Wave gaily o'er the waters brown.   10

And let some graceful arch be there
      With wreathèd mullions proud,
With burnish'd ivy for its screen,
And moss, that glows as fresh and green
      As though beneath an April cloud.—   15

Who says the widow's heart must break,
      The childless mother sink?—
A kinder, truer voice I hear,
Which e'en beside that mournful bier
      Whence parents' eyes would hopeless shrink,   20

Bids weep no more—O heart bereft,
      How strange, to thee, that sound!
A widow o'er her only son,
Feeling more bitterly alone
      For friends that press officious round.   25

Yet is the voice of comfort heard,
      For Christ hath touch'd the bier—
The bearers wait with wondering eye,
The swelling bosom dares not sigh,
      But all is still, 'twixt hope and fear.   30

E'en such an awful soothing calm
    We sometimes see alight
On Christian mourners, while they wait
In silence, by some church-yard gate,
    Their summons to the holy rite.   35

And such the tones of love, which break
    The stillness of that hour,
Quelling th' embitter'd spirit's strife—
"The Resurrection and the Life
    "Am I: believe, and die no more."—   40

Unchang'd that voice—and though not yet
    The dead sit up and speak,
Answering its call; we gladlier rest
Our darlings on earth's quiet breast,
    And our hearts feel they must not break.   45

Far better they should sleep awhile
    Within the Church's shade,
Nor wake, until new heaven, new earth,
Meet for their new immortal birth,
    For their abiding-place be made,   50

Than wander back to life, and lean
    On our frail love once more.
'Tis sweet, as year by year we lose
Friends out of sight, in faith to muse
    How grows in Paradise our store.   55

Then pass, ye mourners, cheerly on,
    Through prayer unto the tomb,
Still, as ye watch life's falling leaf,
Gathering from every loss and grief
    Hope of new spring and endless home.   60

Then cheerly to your work again
    With hearts new-brac'd and set
To run, untir'd, love's blessed race,
As meet for those, who face to face
    Over the grave their Lord have met.   65

2. From Elizabeth Barrett Browning, *Sonnets from the Portuguese* (1850)

[Elizabeth Barrett Browning (1806–61) was, like Tennyson himself, a major figure in the generation of poets who began publishing in the 1830s, at the beginning of the Victorian era. They shared a publisher, and were both leading candidates for the post of poet laureate in 1850, to which Tennyson was ultimately appointed. At birth, the poet's full names were Elizabeth Barrett Moulton-Barrett; in 1845 she married another poet, Robert Browning, and took his last name. Their courtship took place largely by letter; the sequence of 44 *Sonnets from the Portuguese* records it from her point of view. When she and Robert met, Barrett Browning was mourning the recent death of her brother Edward, to which she refers in Sonnet 35; elsewhere in the sequence she refers to her mother's death, which had taken place in 1828. Like *In Memoriam*, *Sonnets from the Portuguese* represents the mourner's finding new objects of love in the wake of bereavement. The sonnets were published in 1850 after the poets' elopement; the title's implication that they are a translation is a blind intended to conceal their deeply personal contents.]

Sonnet 3

Unlike are we, unlike O princely Heart!
Unlike our uses and our destinies.
Our ministering two angels look surprise
On one another, as they strike athwart
Their wings in passing. Thou, bethink thee, art   5
A quest for queens to social pageantries,
With gages from a hundred brighter eyes
Than tears even can make mine, to play thy part
Of chief musician. What hast *thou* to do
With looking from the lattice-lights at me,   10
A poor, tired, wandering singer, singing through
The dark, and leaning up a cypress tree?
The chrism is on thine head,—on mine, the dew,—
And Death must dig the level where these agree.

Sonnet 4

Thou hast thy calling to some palace-floor,
Most gracious singer of high poems! where
The dancers will break footing, from the care
Of watching up thy pregnant lips for more.

And dost thou lift this house's latch too poor 5
For hand of thine? And canst thou think and bear
To let thy music drop here unaware
In folds of golden fulness at my door?
Look up and see the casement broken in,
The bats and owlets builders in the roof! 10
My cricket chirps against thy mandolin.
Hush, call no echo up in further proof
Of desolation! There's a voice within
That weeps ... as thou must sing ... alone, aloof.

Sonnet 18

I never gave a lock of hair away
To a man, Dearest, except this to thee,
Which now upon my fingers thoughtfully,
I ring out to the full brown length and say
"Take it." My day of youth went yesterday; 5
My hair no longer bounds to my foot's glee,
Nor plant I it from rose or myrtle-tree,
As girls do, any more: it only may
Now shade on two pale cheeks the mark of tears,
Taught drooping from the head that hangs aside 10
Through sorrow's trick. I thought the funeral-shears
Would take this first, but Love is justified,—
Take it thou,—finding pure, from all those years,
The kiss my mother left here when she died.

Sonnet 28

My letters! All dead paper, mute and white!
And yet they seem alive and quivering
Against my tremulous hands which loose the string
And let them drop down on my knee to-night.
This said,—he wished to have me in his sight 5
Once, as a friend: this fixed a day in spring
To come and touch my hand ... a simple thing,
Yet I wept for it!—this, ... the paper's light ...
Said, *Dear, I love thee*; and I sank and quailed
As if God's future thundered on my past. 10
This said, *I am thine*—and so its ink has paled
With lying at my heart that beat too fast.
And this ... O Love, thy words have ill availed
If, what this said, I dared repeat at last!

Sonnet 35

If I leave all for thee, wilt thou exchange
And be all to me? Shall I never miss
Home-talk and blessing and the common kiss
That comes to each in turn, nor count it strange,
When I look up, to drop on a new range   5
Of walls and floors, another home than this?
Nay, wilt thou fill that place by me which is
Filled by dead eyes too tender to know change?
That's hardest. If to conquer love, has tried,
To conquer grief, tries more, as all things prove;   10
For grief indeed is love and grief beside.
Alas, I have grieved so I am hard to love.
Yet love me—wilt thou? Open thine heart wide,
And fold within the wet wings of thy dove.

Sonnet 41

I thank all who have loved me in their hearts,
With thanks and love from mine. Deep thanks to all
Who paused a little near the prison-wall
To hear my music in its louder parts
Ere they went onward, each one to the mart's   5
Or temple's occupation, beyond call.
But thou, who, in my voice's sink and fall
When the sob took it, thy divinest Art's
Own instrument didst drop down at thy foot
To hearken what I said between my tears, ...   10
Instruct me how to thank thee! Oh, to shoot
My soul's full meaning into future years,
That *they* should lend it utterance, and salute
Love that endures, from Life that disappears!

Sonnet 44

Belovèd, thou has brought me many flowers
Plucked in the garden, all the summer through
And winter, and it seemed as if they grew
In this close room, nor missed the sun and showers.
So, in the like name of that love of ours,   5
Take back these thoughts which here unfolded too,
And which on warm and cold days I withdrew
From my heart's ground. Indeed, those beds and bowers
Be overgrown with bitter weeds and rue,
And wait thy weeding; yet here's eglantine,   10

Here's ivy!—take them, as I used to do
Thy flowers, and keep them where they shall not pine.
Instruct thine eyes to keep their colours true,
And tell thy soul their roots are left in mine.

3. From Coventry Patmore, *The Angel in the House: The Betrothal* (1854)

[Coventry Patmore (1823–96) was a poet and critic who brought out his first volume in 1844 under the strong influence of Tennyson. The volume did not succeed, but Patmore's admiration for the older poet remained undimmed. After the publication of *In Memoriam*, he embarked on a poetic sequence of his own with married love as the topic. It was published in two parts, under the joint title of *The Angel in the House*: the first part, *The Betrothal*, appeared in 1854 and the second, *The Espousals*, in 1856. A third and fourth part were added later. In 1877 Patmore published a collection of odes, *The Unknown Eros*, and in the following year an important "Essay on English Metrical Law." *The Angel in the House*'s first two parts narrate the courtship and marriage of the protagonists, Felix and Honoria. They are set in an English cathedral town, where Honoria's father is dean. Editions of the poem published later in Patmore's life substantially abridged it; the selections below are drawn from the first edition of *The Betrothal*.]

From Part 1, "The Cathedral Close," Poem 1

Love's Reality

I walk, I trust, with open eyes:
  I've travell'd half my worldly course;
And in the way behind me lies
  Much vanity and some remorse;
I've lived to feel how pride may part   5
  Spirits tho' matched like hand and glove;
I've blush'd for love's abode, the heart,
  But have not disbelieved in love;
And love is my reward; for now,
When most of deadening time complain,   10
  The myrtle is green upon my brow,
Its odour sweet within my brain.

From Part 6, "The Dean," Poem 2

Love Justified

What if my pole-star of respect
　Be dim to others, shall their "Nay,"
Presumably their own defect,
　Invalidate my heart's strong "Yea"?
And can they rightly me condemn,   5
　If I, with partial love, prefer?
I am not more unjust to them,
　But only not unjust to her.
Leave us alone! After awhile,
　This pool of private charity   10
Shall change its shores into an isle,
　And roll a world-embracing sea.
This little germ of nuptial love,
　Which springs so simply from the sod,
The root is, as my Song shall prove,   15
　Of all our love to man and God.

From Part 10, Idyl 10

Going to Church
1.

I woke at three; for I was bid
　To breakfast with the Dean at nine,
And take his girls to Church. I slid
　My curtain, found the season fine,
And could not rest, so rose. The air   5
　Was dark and sharp; the roosted birds
Cheep'd, "Here am I, Sweet; are you there?"
　On Avon's misty flats the herds
Expected, comfortless, the day,
　Which slowly fired the clouds above;   10
The cock scream'd, somewhere far away;
　In sleep the matrimonial dove
Was brooding: no wind waked the wood,
　Nor moved the midnight marish damps,
Nor thrill'd the poplar; quiet stood   15
　The chestnut with its thousand lamps;
The moon shone yet, but weak and drear,
　And seem'd to watch, with bated breath,
The landscape, all made sharp and clear
　By stillness, as a face by death.   20

My prayers for her being done, I took
  Occasion by the quiet hour
To find and know, by Rule and Book,
  The rights of love's beloved power.

3.

Fronting the question without ruth,   25
  Not ignorant that evermore,
If men will stoop to kiss the Truth,
  She lifts them higher than before,
I from above such light required
  As now should once for all destroy   30
. The folly which at times desired
  A sanction for so great a joy.

4.

Thenceforth, and through that prayer, I trod
  A path with no suspicion dim;
I loved her in the name of God,   35
  And for the ray she was of Him;
I ought to admire much more, not less:
  Her beauty was a godly grace:
The mystery of loveliness,
  Which made an altar of her face,   40
Was not the flesh, though that was fair,
  But a most pure and lambent light,
Without a name, by which the rare
  And virtuous spirit flamed to sight.
If oft, in love, effect lack'd cause,   45
  And cause effect, 'twere vain to soar
Reasons to seek for that which was
  Reason itself, or something more.
My joy was no idolatry
  Upon the ends of the vile earth bent,   50
For when I loved her most then I
  Most yearn'd for more divine content,
And felt her charms, less what they were,
  Than what foretold, not slow to infer
How loving and how lovely fair   55
  Must He be who had fashion'd her.
That other doubt, which, like a ghost
  At all love's banquets haunted me,
Was thus resolv'd: Him loved I most,

But her I loved most sensibly: 60
  Lastly, I knew my hope unblamed
By any soil of sensual smirch;
  And forth I went, no whit ashamed
    To take my passion into Church;
Grateful and glad to think that all   65
  Such cogitations would seem vain
To her, whose nature's lighter fall
  Made no divorce 'twixt heart and brain.

5.

I found them, with exactest grace
  And fresh as Spring for Spring attired;   70
And, by the radiance in her face,
  I saw she felt she was admired;
And, through the common luck of love,
  A moment's fortunate delay,
To fit the little lilac glove,   75
  Gave me her arm; and I and they
(They true to this and every hour,
  As if attended on by Time),
Went into Church while yet the tower
  Was warbling with the finish'd chime.   80

6.

Her soft song, singularly heard
  Beside me, in the Psalms, withstood
The roar of voices, like a bird
  Sole singing in a windy wood;
And, when she knelt, she seem'd to be   85
  An angel teaching me to pray;
And all through the sweet Liturgy
  My spirit rejoiced without allay,
Being for once borne clearly above
  All banks and bars of ignorance,   90
By this bright spring-tide of pure love,
  And floated in a free expanse,
Whence it could see from side to side,
  The obscurity from every part
Winnow'd away and purified   95
  By the vibrations of my heart.

7.

The Dean's Text, (oft it happens thus,)
  Most apt to what my thoughts employ'd,
Was Paul's word to those, infamous,
  Of natural affection void.[1]   100
He preach'd but what the conscience saith
  To those blest few that listen well:
"No fruit can come of that man's faith
  Who is to Nature infidel.
God stands not with Himself at strife: 105
  His Work is first, His Word is next:
Two sacred tomes, one Book of Life;
  The comment this, and that the text.
Ill worship they who drop the Creed,
  And take their chance with Jew and Turk;   110
But not so ill as they who read
  The Word, and doubt the greater Work."

---

1 See 2 Timothy 3.3: "Without natural affection, trucebreakers, false accusers,
  incontinent, fierce, despisers of those that are good."

Appendix E: Reviews of In Memoriam, 1850–55

[Nineteenth-century literary reviews were published anonymously; the author identifications supplied here are those of Edgar F. Shannon in his *Tennyson and the Reviewers* (Cambridge, MA: Harvard UP, 1962).]

1. From [John Forster?], *The Examiner* (8 June 1850)

It is a series of poems called forth by the sudden death of a friend; and the nature of the work, as well as the manner in which it would appear to have grown up rather than to have been composed, reminds us of others in their kind as exquisite. We think of Lamb's prose poem on the death of his brother,[1] as the tender beauty of its scenes of anticipated but unrealized happiness breaks upon us. Its classical and philosophical allusions have a family resemblance to *Lycidas*.[2] The number of the poems, and what seems to have been the poet's perseverance year after year in their composition, suggest that in the annals of manly and enduring friendship they may hold the place which in relation to the lover and his mistress is filled by the sonnets of Petrarch.[3] Not thus, however,—nor by comparison even with the extraordinary friendship, love, and grief, commemorated in the sonnets of Shakespeare,—should we commemorate the highest and most distinctive claims of this *In Memoriam*. In the heavenward tone of its thoughts, soaring upward from the earlier and more intense expressions of palsy-stricken grief; in its wayward disconsolate fancies, taming themselves to the calmness of a settled and not overwhelming sorrow; in its vain strivings to connect the Seen and the Unseen, and its final happier anticipations of re-union and existence in higher states of being; the poem receives the elevated tone and character as of a spiritualised, a protestant, a humanitarian *Purgatorio* and *Paradiso*.

---

1 Charles Lamb's essay "Dream Children: A Reverie" (1822) memorializes his brother John.

2 "Lycidas" (1638), John Milton's elegy on the death of Edward King.

3 Petrarch was a Tuscan poet and humanist of the fourteenth century. The songs and sonnets he wrote to his mistress Laura established major conventions of Renaissance love poetry.

2. From *The Literary Gazette* (15 June 1850)

[This review was the only one to mistake the author's gender. Though *In Memoriam* was published anonymously, Tennyson's authorship was an open secret. He had been named as the author on 1 June in the *Publishers' Circular* and in *The Literary Gazette*'s own column of new books.]

A blank title page, but a volume of touching poetry. A fine apostrophe to Love prefaces it, and then it glides into a series of elegiac regret and pathos.... Some one lost by death, in 1833, is lamented on this silver harp, and the tones are instinct with mature and beautiful sorrow.... If by a female hand, as it purports to be, we welcome to the Muses' banquet, melancholy though the music be, one of their sweetest minstrels.

3. From *The North British Review* (August 1850)

In the poem before us we behold the result of many years of self-contemplation and observation of others. Every phrase is the translation to immortality of some hitherto evanescent and unobserved affection; the outward world exists only as a magazine of symbols for revealing the inner world of man; the "subjectivity" is complete; and the result is wholly admirable, for the self-consciousness which, in most modern artists, has served only to intensify selfishness, by offering a thousand fresh and plausible motives to its gratification, has arrived in the author of *In Memoriam*, at a full conviction of the insignificance of self and of the sacred expediency of self-sacrifice.

4. From *The Eclectic Review* (September 1850)

Emerson has shown,[1] how Shakspere,[2] of whom biographically we learn almost *least*, is really most fully known—in his intellectual and spiritual relations to life, and to all about which it nearly concerns us to hear,—of any, merely human, who have ennobled this earth. So, now, one of the most reserved of poets is known to us, in far deeper sense—than would apply to any external biography. Here we have the revelation of the man himself, the picture of his soul during years of

---

1   Ralph Waldo Emerson, American essayist, lecturer, and poet, published the essay "Shakespeare, or the Poet" in his volume *Representative Men* (1850).
2   Based on the poet's signature, this was a common spelling of Shakespeare's name in the eighteenth and nineteenth centuries.

trial and aspiration; with distant glimpses of its glad past, forshadow-ings of its earnest future. Hereby, we are made privy to its inner truth. We learn here, its struggles, yearnings, difficulties, likings; its relations to those cardinal topics having interest for the thoughtful of all time, its views of many pertaining to the present stage of social and intel-lectual change....

[*In Memoriam*] is, throughout, instinct with the freshness of first-feeling. The breeze of early morning plays about it. The spirit of the Dawn informs it. The strong life of those by-gone hours of emotion yet beats here, in earnest pulsations. But, though an early, it is eminently a perfected utterance. Doubtless it has matured, under his hands. Towards the close, matter and manner would indicate some substan-tive interweavings of late date.... In any case, the poem, whether from after maturing, or the elevation to which strong experience raised the poet in the first instance, well represents the Tennyson of to-day, as of yesterday. That experience is now recorded; *past* in all senses, save its gain. This is present in the poet's own being. Much has been solved, much mastered; for him, as for us. On this sure vantage ground of serenity and power, he stands; free for yet nobler enterprise. In its *com-bination* of claims, its personal import, its thoughtful burthen, its art; the *In Memoriam* ranks supreme in interest among his works. It occu-pies a place peculiarly its own, in its poetic and its interpretative value. It is a central member, the key-stone of the rest. By its light we may read them, and the poet too. Personally and poetically, it represents that period, previously a blank to us in his life.

5. From *The English Review* (September 1850)

[The religious objections to *In Memoriam* expressed here reflect *The English Review*'s High Church Anglicanism.]

We have already dwelt with love on the exquisite grace and pathos of a Tennyson, on the passion and power of a Browning; and we have further acknowledged that they, with Mrs. Browning, (late Miss Barrett) may fitly be regarded as the founders of *a new school*, which, though it combines some of the elements of Wordsworth's and of Shelley's poetry, the former's simplicity and the latter's brilliancy, have yet produced effects which are altogether distinct from those of the bards just named; more substantial than Shelley, more concentrated and powerful than Wordsworth. A special mannerism, no doubt, does characterize these living exponents of the beautiful; they are addicted to the use of a certain half-German phraseology, which is not highly to be commended; they are more or less mystical in their utterances, and they very frequently barely suggest where other writers would express; they have sometimes the air of being laboured and artificial just where they have most striven to be plain and natural; they all require to be read more than once before they can be appreciated; their philosophy and religion are somewhat *dubious*. Their feelings indeed are eminently reverential, and their love for Christianity appears sincere; but their opinions would seem by no means formed, and they are more or less wanting in that moral courage, which boldly proclaims its own perception of the truth, without the remotest fear of man's censure or the age's ridicule....

But we are eminently discursive. Waiving all further introduction, let us at once approach the works before us. The first, *In Memoriam*, is a very singular production,—one continuous monody, we may say,— divided into a hundred and thirty separate strains. It is published without an author's name, but every line, every word bears the Tennysonian impress: the whole constitutes a noble monument to the graces, virtues, and powers, never destined to attain maturity, of "A.H.H." (we believe, "Arthur Henry Hallam," the son of the historian), a great friend of Tennyson's....

The poet commences in the dedication (written *last year*, and, therefore, some sixteen springs after the commencement of the series), by addressing himself (to all appearance, at least,) to our Blessed Lord, and imploring His forgiveness for his shortcomings. He commences (it will be observed, that he uses small letters where capitals are now *customary*):—[here the reviewer quotes from *In Memoriam*'s unnumbered first section ll. 1–4, 13–16, 37–44]. Is this Mr. Tennyson's deliberate faith? or are we rather to regard this prayer as the result of a poetic imagination? We know not: certain it is, that if Mr. Tennyson has mustered courage to believe at last (for courage was what was mainly wanting to him!), if he has received revelation as satisfying the highest reason, he has *then* much to answer for in publishing some of the stanzas in this collection, such a poem, for instance, as that ... commencing—"O thou, that after toil and storm," [section 33] in which it is most falsely, and, we may add, offensively assumed, that the unbeliever in Christianity can possess a faith of his own, quite as real and as stable as that of the believer! ...

In other passages the dreams of the author of "Vestiges of Creation" seem to be realized and accepted by the poet, who says, addressing humanity, with reference to its earliest age:—

Arise and fly
The reeling fawn, the sensual feast:
Move upward, *working out the beast*,
And let the ape and tiger die. [Section 118]

But now let us leave this painful theme. We remain undecided as to Mr. Tennyson's faith, though we opine, that, strictly speaking, *he has none*, whether negative or affirmative, and advise him, for his soul's good, to try to get one!

6. From [Charles Kingsley], *Fraser's Magazine* (September 1850)

We are sure, moreover, that the author, whatever right reasons he may have had for concealing his own name, would have no quarrel against us for alluding to it, were he aware of the absolute idolatry with which every utterance of his is regarded by the cultivated young men of our day, especially at the universities, and of the infinite service of which this *In Memoriam* may be to them, if they are taught by it that their superiors are not ashamed of Faith, and that they will rise instead of falling, fulfil instead of denying the cravings of their hearts and intellects, if they will pass upwards with their teacher from the vague though noble expectations of *Locksley Hall*, to the assured and everlasting facts of the proem[1] to *In Memoriam*,—in our eyes, the noblest Christian poem which England has produced for two centuries....

It has been often asked why Mr. Tennyson's great and varied powers have never been concentrated on one immortal work. The epic, the lyric, the idyllic faculties, perhaps the dramatic also, seemed to be all there, and yet all sundered, scattered about in small fragmentary poems. *In Memoriam*, as we think, explains the paradox. Mr. Tennyson could not write an epos or a drama while he was living one. It was true, as people said, that his secluded habits had shut him out from that knowledge of human character necessary for the popular dramatist; but he had been talking all the while with angels. Within the unseen world which underlies and explains this mere time-shadow, which men call Reality and Fact, he had been going down into the depths, and ascending into the heights, led, like Dante of old, by the guiding of a mighty spirit. And in this volume, the record of seventeen years, we have the result of those spiritual experiences in a form calculated, as we believe, to be a priceless benefit to many an earnest seeker in this generation, and perhaps to stir up some who are priding themselves on a cold dilettantism and barren epicurism, into something like a living faith and hope. Blessed and delightful it is to find, that even in these new ages the creeds which so many fancy to be at their last gasp, are still the final and highest succour, not merely of the peasant and the outcast, but of the subtle artist and the daring speculator! Blessed it is to find the most

---

1 Preface or preamble.

cunning poet of our day able to combine the complicated rhythm and melody of modern times with the old truths which gave heart to martyrs at the stake, to see in the science and the history of the nine-teenth century new and living fulfilments of the words which we learnt at our mothers' knee! Blessed, thrice blessed, to find that hero-worship is not yet passed away; that the heart of man still beats young and fresh; that the old tales of David and Jonathan, Damon and Pythias, Socrates and Alcibiades, Shakespeare and his nameless friend, of "love passing the love of woman,"[1] ennobled by its own humility, deeper than death, and mightier than the grave, can still blossom out if it be but in one heart here and there to show men still how sooner or later "he that loveth knoweth God, for God is Love!"[2]

7. From [Manley Hopkins?], *The Times* (28 November 1851)

In turning to consider these verses we will mention on the threshold two leading defects likely, in our opinion, to largely lessen the satis-faction of a reflective and tasteful reader. One is the enormous exag-geration of the grief. We seem to hear of a person unlike ourselves in failings and in virtues. The real fades into the legendary.... The lost friend stalks along a giant of 11 feet, or moves a spiritual being, with an Eden-halo, through life....

A second defect ... is the tone of—may we say so?—amatory ten-derness. Surely this is a strange manner of address to a man, even though he be dead:—

So dearest, now thy brows are cold,
    I see thee what thou art, and know
    Thy likeness to the wise below,
Thy kindred with the great of old.

But there is more than I can see,
    And what I see I leave unsaid,
    Nor speak it, knowing death has made
His darkness beautiful with thee. [Section 74]

---

1 This phrase describes the love of David and Jonathan in 2 Samuel 1:26 ("I am distressed for thee, my brother Jonathan: very pleasant hast thou been unto me: thy love to me was wonderful, passing the love of women"). The other legendary male friendships in Kingsley's list are those of Damon and Pythias, Greek followers of Pythagoras in the fifth century BCE, Socrates and Alcibiades, whose love is narrated in Plato's *Symposium* (ca. 380 BCE), and that of Shakespeare and the young man addressed in the *Sonnets* (1609).

2 See 1 John 4.8 ("He that loveth not knoweth not God; for God is love").

Very sweet and plaintive these verses are; but who would not give them a feminine application? Shakspeare may be considered the founder of this style in English. In Classical and Oriental poetry it is unpleasantly familiar. His mysterious sonnets present the startling peculiarity of transferring every epithet of womanly endearment to a masculine friend,—his master-mistress, as he calls him by a compound epithet, harsh as it is disagreeable.... We object to a Cantab [graduate of Cambridge] being styled a "rose" under any conditions; but do not suppose that we would shut up nature, as a storehouse of imagery and consolation.... We can appreciate the meditative rapture of Burns, who saw his "Jean" in the flower under the hedge; but the taste is displeased when every expression of fondness is sighed out, and the only figure within our view is Amaryllis of the Chancery Bar....[1]

It is not necessary to commend the almost unbroken music of Mr. Tennyson's rhythm—nobody denies his ear. You are sure of a sweet sound, though nothing be in it. We will add that he is extremely successful in the endings of the short poems into which the memorial is broken....

In conclusion, we offer only one observation by way of moral. Small as this book is, it may be abridged with profit.... Whatever be the expansion of ancient song, compression is indispensable to a modern versifier. The circulation of his blood is too languid for a large body and scarcely reaches the extremities. His chances of fame in the future may be calculated by the thickness of his volume. Posterity will only preserve the choicer metal. Epic urns, with their glitter and their baseness, will be broken up, while the ode and the sonnet give forth their little gleams; and he will be the happy rhymer in the coming century, whose grain of gold ... not swollen out with alloy, has melted quite pure into a locket.

8. From [Coventry Patmore], *The Edinburgh Review* (October 1855)

[Patmore initially greeted *In Memoriam* with a much more unambiguously favorable review in *The Palladium*, August 1850. He expresses his second thoughts here in a long essay whose main subject is Tennyson's new poem, *Maud* (1855). In the interim he had written *The Angel in the House,* his own poetic sequence in praise of married love— see Appendix D3 above (p. 187).]

In Memoriam will rank in some respects with Shakspeare's Sonnets, as one of the curiosities of passion, remarkable, not as most great poems

---

1 Amaryllis is a stock name for a shepherdess in pastoral love poetry.

are, for the touch of nature which makes the whole world kin, but for the exceptional feeling which makes the whole world wonder. Nothing but the indubitable and entire sincerity of the feeling, and the simplicity with which it is expressed, could have saved such a work from being charged by most people with extravagance and unfaithfulness to truth. On the majority of those readers who do not read *In Memoriam* as an ordinary 'love poem,' (and, incredible as this may seem, it was in more than one place *reviewed* as such on its first appearance,) this work must necessarily appear as the superlative of love and grief in the wrong place. If so much is said of the affectionate relations of man and man, what, many will naturally ask, remains to be said of that incomparably profounder tenderness which is possible between man and woman? Between boys, or very young men—if such young men there are,—who have never been in love, a passionate and absorbing personal affection, founded generally on a diversity of character so great as to constitute a weak image of the inexhaustible contrast of sex, is not uncommon; though we dissent from Mr. Tennyson when he calls 'first love, first friendship, *equal* powers' [Section 85]; but *In Memoriam* is the expression of no such immature affection as this. It is rather the affection of a man whose sympathies are so abnormally intellectual, and whose intellect is so exceptionally high, that he has as yet failed to find an equal partner for his heart among women.

But thousands of readers, for whom the feeling of this poem has had little meaning, and only an indirect interest, have been attracted by the exposition it contains, or seems to contain, of the poet's religious philosophy. It is a great proof of the depth, sincerity, and simplicity of a man's faith when each sect of religion claims him as its own. The compliment becomes a little too extensive when sceptical philosophy puts in its claim as well. Such, however, is the singular, and most assuredly uncoveted fortune, of the writer of *In Memoriam*. He has gained the hearts of the best thinkers of all the denominations of Christianity by the emphasis of feeling with which he has dwelt, in several of his poems, but particularly in this, upon the simple first foundations of all possible religion, namely, a belief in a personal Divinity, and in

> The head and mighty paramount of truths,
> Immortal life in never fading worlds.[1]

Perhaps from the notion that this very emphasis implies an occasional obscurity of faith, and from a few careless expressions which we our-

---

1 Wordsworth, *The Excursion* 6.85–86.

selves regret, Mr. Tennyson has had the unhappiness to be honoured by some persons as one of the high priests of Pantheism; and others, who have read him with too much understanding and attention to fall into so great a blunder, believe on a more plausible, but still false view of the same grounds, that they have in him at least an impugner of historic Christianity....

Besides these vexatious ambiguities of meaning, there is an absolute defect of taste in such expressions as (speaking of his friend),

> Dear as sacramental wine
> To dying lips is all he said.[1]

And in a less unpleasant way, what can be worse, or more *un-Tennysonian*, than such a periphrasis as

> the kneeling hamlet drains
> *The chalice of the grapes of God.* [Section 10]

These indeed are small, but by no means insignificant spots, in a poem of which the chief characteristics, feminine tenderness and almost matchless grace, are of a nature to make the slightest discord jarring.

The defects of this poem are soon disposed of, but it is difficult to praise its beauties, without falling into the injustice of innumerable omissions, or the insipidity of the vaguest generalities: we must, however, dwell on one quality which seems to us to render this poem an accession of real importance to British classical literature. Although, in some few places, this work wants that perfect polish which distinguishes the author's lesser poems, upon the whole it is not only the best specimen of poetical style which Mr. Tennyson has produced, but it surpasses, in this respect, all poems of equal magnitude written during the past century.

---

1 Section 35. In response to criticism in this review and elsewhere, Tennyson revised "sacramental" to "sacred."

Appendix F: From Hallam Tennyson, Alfred Lord Tennyson: A Memoir by His Son *(1897)*

[Hallam Tennyson (1852–1928) was the elder of Tennyson's two sons and the only one to survive him. From 1874 on he served as his father's secretary, and after the poet's death Hallam edited the Eversley Edition of Tennyson's works, which provides the copy text for this edition, and wrote the *Memoir*, which provides us with the clearest available picture of Tennyson as he wished to be remembered. Hallam's devotion to his father's memory was a mixed blessing for scholarship, as, beside his work as an editor and biographer, it also led him to burn most of Tennyson's letters, including all of those from Arthur Hallam.]

From Vol. 1, Chapter 14, "In Memoriam"

At first the reviews of the volume were not on the whole sympathetic. One critic in a leading journal, for instance, considered that "a great deal of poetic feeling had been wasted," and "much shallow art spent on the tenderness shown to an Amaryllis of the Chancery Bar." Another referred to the poem as follows: "These touching lines evidently come from the full heart of the widow of a military man."[1] However, men like Maurice and Robertson thought that the author had made a definite step towards the unification of the highest religion and philosophy with the progressive science of the day; and that he was the one poet who "through almost the agonies of a death-struggle" had made an effective stand against his own doubts and difficulties and those of the time....

"It must be remembered," writes my father, "that this is a poem, *not* an actual biography. It is founded on our friendship, on the engagement of Arthur Hallam to my sister, on his sudden death at Vienna,

---

1 This passage gives a picture of *In Memoriam*'s reception refracted, one suspects, through 40 years' of the poet's after-dinner narration. In fact the early reviews were overwhelmingly favorable; see Appendix E above. *The Times*'s 1851 reference to Hallam as an "Amaryllis of the Chancery Bar" seems to have stung enough to be remembered verbatim (see Appendix E7, p. 198). No one has ever found a review guessing that the author was a military widow; this sounds like a brilliantly embroidered recollection of the *Literary Gazette*'s mistake immediately after the poem's publication (see Appendix E2, p. 194).

just before the time fixed for their marriage, and on his burial at Cleve-
don Church. The poem concludes with the marriage of my youngest
sister Cecilia. It was meant to be a kind of *Divina Commedia*, ending
with happiness. The sections were written at many different places,
and as the phases of our intercourse came to my memory and sug-
gested them. I did not write them with any view of weaving them into
a whole, or for publication, until I found I had written so many. The
different moods of sorrow as in a drama are dramatically given, and
my conviction that fear, doubts, and suffering will find answer and
relief only through Faith in a God of Love. 'I' is not always the author
speaking of himself, but the voice of the human race speaking thro'
him. After the Death of A.H.H., the divisions of the poem are made
by First Xmas Eve (Section XXVIII), Second Xmas (LXXVIII),
Third Xmas Eve (CIV and CV etc.). I myself did not see Clevedon till
years after the burial of A.H.H. Jan. 3rd, 1834, and then in later edi-
tions of *In Memoriam* I altered the word 'chancel,' which was the word
used by Mr Hallam in his Memoir, to 'dark church.' As to the locali-
ties in which the poems were written, some were written in Lin-
colnshire, some in London, Essex, Gloucestershire, Wales, anywhere
where I happened to be."

Select Bibliography

Editions

Ricks, Christopher, ed. *The Poems of Tennyson*. 3 vols. Berkeley: U of California P, 1987.

Shatto, Susan, and Marion Shaw, eds. *In Memoriam*. Oxford: Oxford UP, 1982.

Tennyson, Hallam, ed. *The Works of Tennyson* ("The Eversley Edition"), 9 vols. London: Macmillan, 1907–08.

Correspondence

Lang, Cecil Y., and Edgar F. Shannon, eds. *The Letters of Alfred Lord Tennyson*. 3 vols. Cambridge, MA: Harvard UP, 1981–90.

Biographies

Martin, Robert Bernard. *Tennyson: The Unquiet Heart*. Oxford: Oxford UP, 1980.

Tennyson, Charles. *Alfred Tennyson*. New York: Macmillan, 1949.

Tennyson, Hallam. *Alfred, Lord Tennyson: A Memoir by His Son*. London: Macmillan, 1897.

Criticism

Adams, James Eli. "Woman, Red in Tooth and Claw." *Victorian Studies* 33.1 (1989): 7–27. Rpt. in Stott, 87–111.

Armstrong, Isobel. *Victorian Poetry: Poetry, Poetics, and Politics*. London and New York: Routledge, 1993.

———. "Tennyson, the Collapse of Subject and Object: *In Memoriam*." *Language as Living Form in Nineteenth-Century Poetry*. Brighton, Sussex: Harvester, 1982, 172–205. Rpt. in Tucker, *Critical Essays on Alfred Lord Tennyson*, 136–52.

Blair, Kirstie. *Victorian Poetry and the Culture of the Heart*. Oxford: Oxford UP, 2006.

Bradley, A.C. *A Commentary on Tennyson's In Memoriam*. 3rd ed. London: Macmillan, 1910.

Cole, Sarah Rose. "The Recovery of Friendship: Male Love and Developmental Narrative in *In Memoriam*." *Victorian Poetry* 50 (2012): 43–66.

Craft, Christopher. "'Descend, and Touch, and Enter': Tennyson's Strange Manner of Address." In Tucker, *Critical Essays on Alfred Lord Tennyson*, 153–73.

Culler, A. Dwight. *The Poetry of Tennyson*. New Haven: Yale UP, 1977.

Dellamora, Richard. *Masculine Desire: The Sexual Politics of Victorian Aestheticism*. Chapel Hill: U of North Carolina P, 1990.

Eliot, T.S. "In Memoriam." *Essays Ancient and Modern*. London: Faber and Faber, 1936. Rpt. in Killham, 207–15.

Hair, Donald. *Domestic and Heroic in Tennyson's Poetry*. Toronto: U of Toronto P, 1981.

——. *Tennyson's Language*. Toronto: U of Toronto P, 1991.

Killham, John, ed. *Critical Essays on the Poetry of Tennyson*. London: Routledge and Kegan Paul, 1960.

Nunokawa, Jeff. "*In Memoriam* and the Extinction of the Homosexual," *ELH* 58.2 (1991): 427–38. Rpt. in Stott, 197–209.

Peltason, Timothy. *Reading In Memoriam*. Princeton: Princeton UP, 1985.

Ricks, Christopher. *Tennyson*. New York: Macmillan, 1972.

Rowlinson, Matthew. "The Thing in the Poem: *Maud*'s Hymen." *differences* 12.3 (2001): 128–65.

Sacks, Peter M. *The English Elegy: Studies in the Genre from Spenser to Yeats*. Baltimore: Johns Hopkins UP, 1985.

Shaw, W. David. *Tennyson's Style*. Ithaca: Cornell UP, 1976.

Sinfield, Alan. *The Language of Tennyson's In Memoriam*. Oxford: Blackwell, 1971.

——. *Alfred Tennyson*. Oxford: Blackwell, 1986.

Stott, Rebecca, ed. *Tennyson*. London and New York: Longman, 1996.

Tucker, Herbert F. *Tennyson and the Doom of Romanticism*. Cambridge, MA: Harvard UP, 1988.

——, ed. *Critical Essays on Alfred Lord Tennyson*. New York: G.K. Hall, 1993.

from the publisher

A name never says it all, but the word "broadview" expresses a good deal of the philosophy behind our company. We are open to a broad range of academic approaches and political viewpoints. We pay attention to the broad impact book publishing and book printing has in the wider world; we began using recycled stock more than a decade ago, and for some years now we have used 100% recycled paper for most titles. As a Canadian-based company we naturally publish a number of titles with a Canadian emphasis, but our publishing program overall is internationally oriented and broad-ranging. Our individual titles often appeal to a broad readership too; many are of interest as much to general readers as to academics and students.

Founded in 1985, Broadview remains a fully independent company owned by its shareholders—not an imprint or subsidiary of a larger multinational.

If you would like to find out more about Broadview and about the books we publish, please visit us at **www.broadviewpress.com**. And if you'd like to place an order through the site, we'd like to show our appreciation by extending a special discount to you: by entering the code below you will receive a 20% discount on purchases made through the Broadview website.

Discount code: **broadview20%**

Thank you for choosing Broadview.

Please note: this offer applies only to sales of bound books within the United States or Canada.

The interior of this book is printed on 100% recycled paper.